J.-B. Say

———————————————

J.-B. Say

AN ECONOMIST IN TROUBLED TIMES

Writings selected and translated by

R. R. *Palmer*

PRINCETON UNIVERSITY PRESS

PRINCETON, NEW JERSEY

Copyright © 1997 by Princeton University Press
Published by Princeton University Press, 41 William Street,
Princeton, New Jersey 08540
In the United Kingdom: Princeton University Press,
Chichester, West Sussex

Library of Congress Cataloging-in-Publication Data

Say, Jean-Baptiste, 1767–1832
An economist in troubled times : writings / selected and
translated by R.R. Palmer
  p. cm.
Includes bibliographical references and index
ISBN 0-691-01170-2 (cloth : alk. paper)

1. Say, Jean-Baptiste, 1767–1832. 2. Economics.
3. Economics—France—History—Sources.
4. Economists—France—Correspondence.
I. Palmer, R. R. (Robert Roswell), 1909–
HB105.S25A25   1997
330—dc20   96-25412   CIP

This book has been composed in Galliard

Princeton University Press books are printed
on acid-free paper and meet the guidelines
for permanence and durability of the Committee
on Production Guidelines for Book Longevity
of the Council on Library Resources

Printed in the United States of America

1 3 5 7 9 10 8 6 4 2

For Esther, as always

———————————

CONTENTS

Introduction   3

CHAPTER ONE
The Mild Revolutionary   6

Freedom of Speech
Journalism
Benjamin Franklin
Bureaucracy
The Theater
The Constitution of 1795
Promoting the Arts and Trades

CHAPTER TWO
The Sober Utopian   33

A Moral Society
Plain Living and Comfort
The Need for Political Economy
Monuments and Aphorisms

CHAPTER THREE
The Frustrated Economist   46

The French in Egypt
Offending Napoleon
Political Economy as a Science
Everybody's Business
Elementary Schools for All
Extravagance and Deprivation
The Profits and Evils of Slavery

CHAPTER FOUR
The Innovative Economist   66

Utility and Value
Goods and Services
The Entrepreneur
Say's Law
Population
Say in Business for Himself
Emigration? Thomas Jefferson

CHAPTER FIVE

The Commentator on England   90

British Wealth and Credit
Taxes, Debt, Deficit, and Poverty
Machinery and Steam Engines
Paper Money: The Bank of England
India and the East India Company
Ireland and Its Future
Assisted Emigration
The University of London

CHAPTER SIX

The Professor of Political Economy   117

Economics for Entrepreneurs
Critique of Contemporaries
The Canal Age
Liberia
The Uses of Statistics
Economics and the Fate of Nations
The Chair at the College of France

References   157

Index   165

J.-B. Say

———————————

INTRODUCTION

JEAN-BAPTISTE SAY is most commonly remembered, when at all, as a disciple of Adam Smith and in particular as the author of what later economists have called Say's Law. He was in fact much more; he modified and extended some of Adam Smith's insights, became a friend and correspondent of Thomas Malthus and David Ricardo, formulated Say's Law with qualifications often overlooked, and at the end of his life, in 1832, was the first professor of political economy in France. His life coincided with two great revolutions, the French Revolution with its long aftermath and the Industrial Revolution in Great Britain, on both of which he had much to say. He is exceptional among economists in that for several years he was in business for himself as a factory owner and so took part in the activities that he and other economists analyzed. Anyone interested in any of these subjects may enjoy reading the present book, for he always wrote in nontechnical language for a thoughtful but unspecialized audience. The variety of his concerns is shown in our Table of Contents.

He insisted that political economy, as economics was then called, was a true science but as such was also a moral science, since it involved the goals and motivations of human beings. It merged into what are now called both the social sciences and the humanities. He saw no sharp difference between facts and values, since values were among the facts of human behavior. Political economy and political science, although distinct, were also overlapping. He held that the most productive economy must rest on private property, private enterprise, and private incentives, in which "private" meant not controlled by the state, but for which a strong state and reliable legal system were necessary; and he held also that a free and representative government assuring individual rights ("democracy") could only be maintained by a productive economy from which all social classes received a fair but not equal share in the output. He once remarked that political economy might better have been called "social economy," and was a believer in what has been somewhat pompously known as interdisciplinary cross-fertilization.

Various of Say's writings were translated into fourteen languages within his lifetime. His principal work, *A Treatise on Political Economy*, first appeared in French in 1803, but it was suppressed by Napoleon and did not appear in English. It has been known to some Anglophone scholars, but its rarity even in French and the difficulties it presents for others may justify inclusion here of passages from it among the selected writings of J.-B. Say. Its fourth edition of 1821 was immediately trans-

lated into English, after which there were twenty-eight reprintings over
the next sixty years. These reprintings were all in the United States, and
are enough to suggest the influence of Say on the study and teaching of
economics in the United States in the nineteenth century. The translation had in fact been made in England, but the British apparently felt
less continuing need for such an import, having their own economists in
Say's predecessor Adam Smith and his contemporaries Malthus and Ricardo. As both a follower and a critic of Adam Smith, whom he often
quoted, and in close touch with Malthus and Ricardo, he is universally
regarded as one of the luminaries of classical economics. As a classic, his
Treatise was reprinted again in English in 1964, and in French in 1972
and 1982. There is now a certain timeliness in his views on the advantages of a free market over other economic arrangements.

Of Say's writings presented here none has ever been translated into
English, with a few exceptions to be noted later. In this book the first
two chapters contain a miscellany of pieces written in Paris during the
Revolution until 1800, in some of which we can detect signs of the future economist. The next two revolve about the *Treatise* in its hitherto
untranslated edition of 1803, from which in the third chapter excerpts
are chosen to show how the *Treatise* may have displeased Napoleon, and
in the fourth chapter to present some of his new contributions to economic thought. The fifth chapter assembles his views on England and
Scotland in and after 1814, and the sixth is made up of various items
written during his final years as an established economist. American
readers may especially note his fascination with Benjamin Franklin, his
correspondence with Jefferson and thoughts of emigrating to America,
his interest in the Erie Canal, and his typically European ambivalence toward the United States in his mixture of admiration for American freedom, repugnance for its black slavery, and warnings against excessive
concern for money-making and material satisfactions.

Historians of economic thought, such as J. A. Schumpeter and others
cited in the references below, have generally praised Say but found him
wanting in analytical rigor. This very quality may make him more understandable to uninitiated readers. He wrote his *Treatise* for a wider audience than other economists, and also produced many lighter or occasional pieces. Living through the French Revolution and the years of
Napoleon, with their twenty-three years of war, observing the industrial
revolution in Britain, and surviving the restored Bourbon monarchy
until his death in 1832, he had opinions on political and social as well as
more purely economic questions.

The Says were an old Protestant family originally from southern
France. When Louis XIV put an end to the toleration of Protestantism,
in 1685, Jean-Baptiste Say's great-grandfather had moved to Switzer-
land and settled in Geneva. Say's father was born in Geneva in 1739, but

as life became somewhat easier for Protestants in France he returned there about 1760 and became a silk merchant in Lyon, where Jean-Baptiste was born in 1767. The young Say had a good schooling in Lyon, including attention to the natural sciences and other modern subjects, and was then sent by his father for a two-year sojourn in England to learn business practice in London and gain facility in the English language. Meanwhile, his parents moved to Paris, where Jean-Baptiste joined them about 1787. He found employment in Paris with an insurance company conducted by Etienne Clavière, a Protestant banker and refugee from political troubles in Geneva who was to play a significant role in the French Revolution. Clavière possessed a copy of Adam Smith's *Wealth of Nations* in English, which he gave his young employee to read. Say read it with ease, having been long in England, and also with profit and admiration, so much so that he ordered from London a copy for himself, which he covered with notes.

Thus, when the revolution began, the young Say, twenty-two years old in 1789, was well motivated to accept the changes it brought and to become a thinker on economic questions. With the business background of his family and his own association with businessmen in London and Paris, he had reason to favor what has been called the "bourgeois" revolution, and as a Protestant he could only welcome the final removal of disabilities from which Protestants had suffered. Never active in the Revolution, he also never opposed it, even during the Terror, and his later writings are free from the retrospective lamentations in which even liberals indulged. He also remembered his first reading of Adam Smith as his initiation into the problems of political economy.

Chapter One

THE MILD REVOLUTIONARY

SAY'S WRITINGS during the Revolution were all brief and ephemeral. They consist only of a pamphlet on the freedom of the press published early in 1789, and of contributions to a periodical called the *Décade philosophique*, a journal launched in 1794 at the height of the Terror by a group of intellectuals for whom Say became a junior associate. His activity, as distinct from writing, was of little importance. There is no evidence, or later hint, that he ever took part in any political demonstration or joined any political club. Through his mentor and employer, Clavière, he became one of Mirabeau's helpers in 1790 and 1791, and when Clavière served as finance minister for a short time in 1792 Say was on the margin of politics. With the outbreak of war in 1792 he served a few months in a battalion of volunteers. Returning to his normal life, he was married in May 1793 to Julie de Loche, the daughter of a successful lawyer, and the marriage proved to be long-lasting and happy; it also excused him from the famous *levée en masse* of the following August, which called all able men and women to action against the foreign invaders but exempted young married men from military service. By 1798 he was old enough to be unaffected by the more systematic conscription law of that year, by which only men under twenty-six were drafted.

He wrote the pamphlet of 1789 at some time before the meeting of the Estates-General in May, the conventional date for the beginning of the Revolution. Hundreds of other pamphlets had appeared since the preceding summer, debating how the coming Estates should meet, whether in three separate houses for clergy, nobles, and Third Estate or in a single body, how delegates should be selected, how they should be instructed by their constituencies, and much else, including the prospect of a new constitution. Say's pamphlet makes no mention of any of these matters. The government had made erratic attempts to control such outpourings, but without success. A freedom of the press existed *de facto* at the moment, but not *de jure* with any assurance of permanence.

Say's pamphlet therefore treated a relevant and important subject. The author shares warmly in the high hopes of the time, believing that the king and everyone else wanted the same things. We can hear the voice of a recent reader of Adam Smith when he observes that France "produces" ideas which by "exchange" can multiply to the advantage of all concerned. But there is a note of caution; his most distinctive point is to suggest how *abuses* of press freedom may be prevented.

After opening with respectful thanks and congratulations to the good king and his ministers for their part in the regeneration of the country, he addresses the public in the language of the day:

> . . . And as for us, my fellow-citizens, let us congratulate one another. Let us burst with joy and even pride in being no longer inhabitants of a despotic state but members of a respectable nation, knowing that henceforth the virtues and talents of each of us will combine for the happiness of all.
>
> Let us no longer enchain those useful virtues and talents. Let us circulate in France the ideas that France produces, so that each of us may have his necessary share. Yes, necessary, for the light of the mind is like the light of day. It no sooner penetrates our houses than our work, pleasures and movements all come alive; and hence comes happiness. But if the light fails us, or if we close up its passage, then we fall asleep; and sleep is the moral equivalent of barbarism. Who would wish to retrogress to the reign of Charles VI [king of France, 1380–1422] and go back to that unformed state of human existence?
>
> We were saved from it by the invention of printing. By printing it became possible for a man to speak to all times and countries; and by an easy exchange of ideas everyone is enriched. Two men may each have one idea; by exchange each has two; and by the thousand voices of the press they are communicated to a hundred thousand persons.
>
> Unfortunately, nothing effective is without abuses; and the abuses that seem to flow from a free use of the press have always alarmed even those most persuaded of its great advantages.
>
> It is mainly to such persons that I address myself.
>
> I will not try to demonstrate how freedom of the press is favorable to letters, civilization, the government of states, and to a salutary philosophy that softens manners and leads to tolerance and humanity. I would only risk saying what everyone thinks. . . . I will look for the means of reducing the disadvantages and abuses of this freedom. . . .
>
> Thought is destined to fly from one mind to another, and no one has the right to stop it. Yet among us, and in our time, a man of genius must still submit his broad conceptions to the compass of a censor, who may be inept and is always self-interested and timid.
>
> The censor fears that he may be too lenient, and so is strict about trifles. He is afraid of missing an allusion or hidden meaning, and so comes to strange interpretations. He is afraid that through inattention

he has overlooked some reprehensible phrase; and so to be safe he bans the whole work, for the censor runs risks by approving a book but no risk by rejecting it.

And when a writer is willing to face these obstacles, think of the unpleasant actions he must take! He has to work nights and lose time and the right moment for publication. Sometimes he cuts a passage, or sometimes adds one, and so obscures the clarity of his expression to the point of insignificance. Or he is obliged to flatter, to know how to deal with a despotic judge; and nevertheless, despite this humiliating precaution, a single idea displeasing to the judge brings disgrace on the entire book, and the thoughts and labors of several years are lost by a caprice. . . .

[Such obstacles] drive into foreign countries a branch of commerce that could enrich our kingdom, for without them France, whose language is known everywhere and which is justly celebrated for its stores of knowledge, could become both the school and the library of Europe. . . .

There is fear of abuses. Let us see what they are, and look for remedies to this evil.

To write is to speak to the eyes. It is to use different signs to express the same ideas, but it is easier to abuse some signs than others. A man is personally responsible for what he says, but an unknown scribbler delivers what he has written, and then hides himself. The problem is to make the man who writes as circumspect as the one who speaks, and the obvious way to do this is to require every author to make himself known. But what recourse would there then be for one who for modesty or some other reason feels he must remain anonymous? Let us preserve this recourse.

Since no one should make a statement of which he might be ashamed, or which he would wish to deny, let us create a tribunal to represent in France that ideal nation called the Republic of Letters, which, under this remarkable name, adopted by all civilized peoples, expresses very well the general opinion on the freedom to be given to thoughtful minds. This tribunal, sanctioned by the public confidence, would elect a secretary to be the sole depository and guarantee of an author's secrecy. Authors would be obliged, *by law*, to declare themselves to this secretary on delivering their work to the printer.

It is before this tribunal that any simple citizen or government minister could bring complaint against a printed work. Here I could denounce an audacious libel or demand an accounting for what is said against me, my family, my king, or my country. If the judges found my complaint justified they would summon the author to defend himself, and decide between us.

Say says nothing on what penalty an author would pay if this tribunal decided against him, or what would happen if an anonymous author had refused to register his name with the tribunal. He goes on to give further assurance to the conservatively minded:

> Having shown that a free press is no more dangerous to society than a press subject to restraints, I must admit that this is not enough. Some will wish me to prove that this liberty is consistent with the authority of government. By a deduction as barbarous as it is false they may decide in advance that if authority is to be maintained liberty must be proscribed.
>
> With freedom of the press established it will still be a crime to reveal the secrets of councils, to slander men in office, or to decry acts of government for which the motives cannot be known. Such crimes should be publicly punished, and all the more abhorred so far as everyone has an interest in the political regime. We are now at a moment when stable laws, consented to by the nation, are about to sanction legitimate authority. The man who would attack such authority would be attacking the work of the nation; he would be arraigning France itself.

We have here Say's only reference in this pamphlet to a constitution yet to be written, by which the will of the nation was to endow government with legitimacy. Whether or not reassuring to conservatives in 1789, much the same words could also have been used by Robespierre a few years later. The doctrine of 1793 held that the National Convention was a legitimate government, elected by the people and expressing the will of the nation in time of war and revolution, and so to be protected from slander and from ignorant or malicious misunderstanding. Possibly Say himself had some such feeling in 1793 and 1794, or belief that the then government of France, under the Convention's Committee of Public Safety, was more legitimate than any likely alternative at the moment. Even mild revolutionaries wanted no counterrevolution imposed by victorious foreign powers.

The pamphlet concludes with an optimistic peroration:

> O you who make laws, make them to prevent abuses, and no more. In the name of him who gave us the priceless gift of speech, let men speak! If justice and public order demand punishment for the person who calumniates, who wrongs another in words, who criminally undermines a legitimately established order, let such a person be the only one to be punished! And since to print is only to speak more loudly, so as to be heard by a greater number, do not tie the hand that traces signs more than the tongue that voices sounds. . . .
>
> Then, how many ideas will be expressed! If useless, they will be for-

gotten; if harmful, they will be scorned; but those that are beneficial will germinate, prosper, and spread among us all the good things that a perfected human spirit can produce.

Nothing came from this pamphlet of 1789, or from Say's ideas for preventing the abuses of anonymous authorship. The press continued to be free as the Revolution gathered strength, and it produced mainly not what Say had hoped for, but a proliferation of belligerent pamphleteering and journalism which expressed all shades of opinion to advance or reverse the ongoing movement. One such journal, or political newspaper, was the *Courrier de Provence* of the comte de Mirabeau, a prominent revolutionary leader in 1789 who by the time of his death in 1791 expressed a preference for a strong constitutional monarchy. Say worked for Mirabeau, but his role in production of the journal was incidental and ceased with Mirabeau's death. He could hardly have been encouraged by what happened next. War began in April 1792, Paris was threatened by invading armies, a revolutionary insurrection in August unseated Louis XVI, a new National Convention was elected, and France became a republic. Louis XVI was put to death in January 1793; the revolutionary vanguard divided; and the National Convention, threatened by another popular armed insurrection, expelled twenty-nine of its members, known as Girondins, on June 2, 1793. Among them was Say's patron, Clavière, who committed suicide in prison.

Say, recently married, was at this time living in the country and planning to open a school. He seemed willing enough to keep apart from the mounting fury, but he was approached by a group of writers who proposed to found a new journal, to be called the *Décade philosophique, littéraire et politique*. Some of the group had been associated with Mirabeau or Clavière. They were republicans of the kind that hoped for a peaceable, stable, prosperous, enlightened, and generally middle-class republic to follow the crisis of the moment—what Bonaparte would later call the *idéologues*. Busy themselves with other concerns, they were looking for a younger man to take on the daily operation of their new journal, be in effect its editor, and write occasional contributions. The word *Décade* referred to the ten-day "week" of the recently introduced republican calendar. The *Décade* would be a "weekly," and to manage it would be a demanding job.

Say accepted their invitation. He also became one of six coproprietors of the *Décade* and the print shop that published it. The first number appeared on 10 Floréal of the Year II of the Republic, or April 29, 1794. Say continued at this editorial post for five years, through the period of the Directory that followed the Convention, and until Napoleon Bonaparte took over the government late in 1799. Three of his colleagues became members of the National Institute when it was established in 1795, and two of these were in its Class in Moral and Political Sciences. This category included *économie politique*, under which heading the *Décade* published articles and short reviews, of which only a minority were by J.-B. Say.

The first three months of Say's editorship coincided with the climax of the Terror. And the curious fact is that his most notable achievement during the Terror was to publicize and praise the life and writings of Benjamin Franklin.

The memory of Franklin in France was highly respected and noncontroversial. On news of his death in 1790 he had been eulogized in an oration by Mirabeau in the National Assembly. His scientific work had been admired in France since the 1750s. He had lived in France from 1777 to 1785, during the War of American Independence when France was allied to the revolutionary United States. As a seventy-year-old diplomat in Paris he had created a sensation in the fashionable and literary world of the French capital. The image of the printer from Philadelphia, the homely philosopher, the great man of science and famous statesman suited the purposes of the *Décade philosophique* in 1794 very well. At a time when it was dangerous to comment on current affairs, and when even one of the proprietors of the *Décade*, P. L. Ginguené, was arrested (though for reasons unrelated to that journal), the image of Franklin could be made to project the orderly virtues that the owners of the *Décade* wanted the French Republic some day to embody.

In the summer of 1794, shortly before the overthrow of Robespierre, the same shop that printed the *Décade philosophique*, owned by Say and his partners, produced also a book entitled *La science du Bonhomme Richard*. The French word *science* could mean any form of sound knowledge, and *bonhomme* meant a simple, good-natured fellow. The book, in short, presented a translation of Franklin's *Poor Richard's Almanac*. It included also an account of the interrogation of Franklin by the House of Commons at the time of the Stamp Act in 1766. Both Poor Richard and the interrogation had been published in France as long ago as 1777, during the American war. At that time the questioning of Franklin in parliament, by showing the disdain of English aristocrats for their colonial subjects, could be used as propaganda against Great Britain. A reprinting in 1794 served the same wartime purpose. But this new reprinting was introduced by an *abrégé de la vie de Franklin* written by Jean-Baptiste Say.

Say's *abrégé*, or condensed life, forms part of a complex web from which what we know as the *Autobiography of Benjamin Franklin* later emerged. Franklin himself had written his autobiography in fragments at various times, but these fragments reached only as far as the year 1759,

the fifty-third year of his age. For his career after 1759 there existed in
Say's time a number of narratives or summaries written by others, some
in print and some only in manuscript, which traced the most politically
significant part of Franklin's life, including the fourteen years in England, the eight years in France, and his membership in the bodies that
issued the Declaration of Independence and the Constitution of the
United States. It is not clear on what sources Say drew for his own
abrégé. Most of it he puts in quotation marks, without indication of authorship. Only the latter part of the *abrégé* is of Say's own composition,
picking up at about the year 1750. After taking note of Franklin's elec-
trical experiments, his famous kite, his invention of the lightning rod,
and the Franklin stove, Say goes on to the political part of his story. He
tells again what had already become the legend of Benjamin Franklin. In
Say's version there is no mention of the Declaration of Independence or
the new Constitution of the United States. But for his French readers of
1794 he makes Franklin (very erroneously) into a revolutionary activist
some twenty years before the American Revolution.

> . . . The ministry in England was aware of Franklin's ascendancy and
> feared his influence. In keeping with their corrupt system, they thought
> that, by granting him one of the lucrative employments in the colonies
> that they had at their disposal, they would win over his interest for
> keeping the Americans under their yoke. He was appointed [in 1753]
> *director general of the post office in British America*. But he made no
> effort to flatter the power to which he owed this office; he thought only
> of developing an institution so favorable to the communication of
> ideas, human contacts, and commercial activity. He understood that his
> work on such matters would itself accelerate the liberation of America.
> Since his position authorized him to travel continually in all parts of the
> colonies without arousing suspicions in the home government, he used
> it to explore the state of opinion, guide it wisely, prudently heighten
> the horror felt for oppression, and so effortlessly to promote the ten-
> dencies toward independence. A few sensible and unforgettable words,
> spoken in conversation with other travelers at inns during the evening,
> or to crowds of patriots that gathered to see him, were enough for him
> to spread at every step the seeds of resistance to oppression.
> Men and things being in this condition, he was sent by the assembly
> of Pennsylvania to England [in 1764] to defend the interests of the col-
> onies against the court. He concealed nothing and gained nothing
> from the ministers. Summoned before the bar of parliament, he carried
> in himself the dignity of a whole people soon to be born to indepen-
> dence. Without knowing in advance the questions that would be put to
> him, he simply presented himself with his own native genius. He was

inspired by truth and by liberty. In his answers there were no vague ideas or useless words. He expressed simple ideas, broad views and generous sentiments.

At this point Say has a footnote, reminding the reader that an account of this interrogation by the House of Commons is to be found later in the same volume.

In short, both while he was in London and after his return to America, by his printed writings, private correspondence, numerous connections and incredible activity, he can be regarded as the principal promoter of the American revolution. But he was strongly supported by Adams and Washington.

A congress was formed, and Franklin sat in it. It decided for liberty. All obstacles that might block the first steps were skillfully removed; all precautions that might assure success were taken in advance. The organization of citizen troops, their pay, their instructions, all the military details written in Franklin's hand and deposited in the archives of Philadelphia, testify to the breadth and foresight of his thinking.

When war began he was sent by the United States to solicit aid from France by finishing the negotiation begun by Dean. He left without money, for his country had none. He arrived in Paris with a cargo of tobacco, as once the deputies of Holland, hoping for freedom, had arrived in Brussels with a shipment of herrings to pay their expenses. He landed at Nantes on December 16, 1776, proceeded to Paris, and was lodged at Passy. His whole manner announced the simplicity of olden times. He had left off wearing a wig, and showed the amazed multitude a head worthy of the brush of Guido on an erect and vigorous body clothed in the simplest garments. He wore large spectacles, and carried a white staff. He spoke little; he could be unpolished without rudeness, and his pride was no more than the sense of his own dignity. Such a person was made to excite the curiosity of Paris; people trooped to see him pass in the streets; they asked each other who this old peasant with such a noble air was, and repeatedly heard the answer: *It is the famous Franklin!*

For a year the French ministry showed a very reserved attitude toward him, but with the defeat of General Burgoyne at Saratoga. . . it recognized the independence of the United States and the mission of Franklin—of Franklin the candle maker who had been a printer's apprentice, homeless and unknown in Philadelphia, munching a piece of dry bread in the street while he looked for work. This important example is one of the finest triumphs of Equality; it opened our eyes and led to the establishment of our own august Republic.

Franklin returned to America in September 1785. . . . A crowd of citizens accompanied him to his home with shouts of joy, while bells and cannon announced the event in the open country. The people of Phila- delphia heaped their marks of esteem and veneration upon him. The congress, the university and various societies presented addresses ex- pressing their affection, and he was elected governor of Pennsylvania, an office that he held for three years. Finally, on April 17, 1790, he left this world where he had done only good, followed by the benedictions of his countrymen and leaving a name revered by all good and enlight- ened men, a name that recalls none but agreeable memories.

The volume containing this condensed life of Franklin, together with Poor Richard and the interrogation, was reviewed anonymously in the *Décade* on 30 Thermidor of the Year II (August 17, 1794), three weeks after the death of Robespierre. It is highly probable that the anonymous reviewer was Say himself, reviewing and thus advertising a book which he and his colleagues had brought into being. Not only was the book produced in the same print shop as produced the *Décade*, but we know from one of Say's letters at this time that he was getting little help from his coproprietors and was doing most of the work himself. His later writ- ings show a sustained interest in Franklin that may have originated in 1794. He would quote Poor Richard's maxims approvingly in both his utopia of 1800 and his *Treatise on Political Economy* in its first and later editions.

The following are excerpts from the review of Thermidor of the Year II. The reviewer depicts an imaginary scene with a character called Fa- ther Abraham, created by Franklin himself as a vehicle to convey a col- lection of his aphorisms published in Philadelphia in 1758.

We find in this work the maxims, or moral axioms, that form part of the reputation of Franklin. *Poor Richard's Almanac* is a masterpiece of common sense, concision, and simplicity, to which one might almost add subtlety, if so discredited a word could be applied to the most lofty as well as the most useful conceptions of both private and political economy.

"If you love life waste no time," says Poor Richard, "because time is what life is made of." Such is Poor Richard's style. But who is this Poor Richard? He is only a maker of almanacs. One day when he was riding his horse (proving that in the United States an almanac maker can have a horse and ride it) he came to a place where an outdoor sale of a mer- chant's goods was to be held, and where consequently a large crowd was assembled. The sale had not yet begun, and everyone was talking about the government, public affairs, the bad weather, and similar mat- ters. Among them was an old man known as Father Abraham, who seemed the most important person in the group. People turned to him and asked his advice. Abraham, after thinking for a moment, launched into a long discourse in which he made the most useful economic and moral ideas understandable to the most obtuse minds. But what was remarkable in this speech was that he kept quoting Poor Richard at every turn.

Richard, sitting on his horse to listen, was so delighted, and so really delighted, that he remained until the end to hear himself quoted.

Abraham showed his hearers the way to meet the demands of government for taxes and still be well and happy. "Idleness makes everything difficult," he said quoting Poor Richard, "and industry makes everything easy." "He who gets up late in the morning is troubled all day, and has hardly begun his business by nightfall." "Laziness moves so slowly that poverty soon catches up." "Do you have something to do tomorrow? Do it today." . . . "It costs more to support one vice than to raise two children." . . . "Fools give big dinners and wise men eat them."

He shows that from not having read Poor Richard they may have come to this sale looking for what are called *bargains*. He says that what is not necessary is always dear. Poor Richard says, "I have seen many people ruined by good bargains."

. . . Such are the writings of the ambassador of the United States to France. Nothing touching the interests of humanity was beneath him. He had read much, experienced much, and knew how to observe. Hence there are few books containing so much in so small a space. We constantly find words that impress by their truth, their brevity, and their insight. "Experience keeps a school that teaches hard lessons, but the only school where the slow-witted can learn." And elsewhere: "If you will not listen to reason it will still make itself felt."

After Poor Richard the reader finds in this book the famous interrogation of Franklin at the bar of the British parliament. . . .

Here the reviewer, if it was Say, as seems likely, restates what he had said in the condensed life introducing the book.

To return to the interrogation. We find here some curious and truly historic ideas on America before the revolution, on its population, resources and customs. But what has most struck us in reading it is that we see in the parliament of that time the same principles, and the same delusions, as its majority has revealed more recently. It wished to have the influence on the United States that it now wishes to have on the government and opinions of the French. The ministry and its dependents went to extremes in trying to preserve a power that was about to escape them. A great revolution, the liberation of America, was going forward slowly and irresistibly. If the same symptoms are now appearing in England in the desperation of its ministry, the debasement of its parliament, and the delirious pride of its government, and are in general reappearing now precisely as they did then, and are reaching new heights, what are we to conclude? That England is on the eve of one of those political shocks, or great perturbations, that the most astute ministers will never be able to suppress.

It must be remembered that France and Britain were at war, that British money was financing Continental armies, and British agents penetrating the peasant and royalist rebellion in western France, so that even mild revolutionaries could hope that the British government might soon collapse, especially since it could also be believed that the English were a freedom loving people.

Once again, in 1798, as editor of the *Décade philosophique*, Say had occasion to present Benjamin Franklin as a model. In fourteen pages of the number for 30 Pluviôse of the Year VI he included a fragment of Franklin's autobiography which had never yet been published. It was a fragment written by Franklin in Paris in 1784, dealing with his life half a century before in 1731. Franklin on returning to America had left a manuscript copy with a French friend, from whom it somehow came into the hands of the owners of the *Décade*. Probably it was Say with his knowledge of English who translated the fragment. Its appearance in French in the *Décade* was the first publication of it in any language. It is one of the best known passages in the autobiography, in which Franklin tells how as a young man he had set up a list of thirteen virtues, accompanied by a blank form on which he recorded his progress, if any, in each of these virtues from day to day. Say presented it with no comment or explanation, so that he cannot be quoted, but a few of Franklin's own words suggest why a future economist might find the fragment significant. Franklin wrote (as retrotranslated from the *Décade*'s French), naming five of the thirteen virtues in italics:

> It may be useful to my posterity to know that this little artifice [the table of virtues] was the source, with God's help, of the continuing happiness of their ancestor's life until his seventy-ninth year, when this is written. The adversities that may mark the rest of his days are in the hands of Providence, but if troubles come the remembrance of his past happiness should help him to support them with resignation. He attributes to *sobriety* his long continuing health and what remains to him of a good constitution; to *application* and *economy* the financial comfort he obtained in his early years and the acquisition of the fortune and knowledge that enabled him to become a useful citizen and brought him some reputation among the learned; to *sincerity* and *justice* the confidence of his country and the honorable employments with which he has been charged.

A few months later a new *Vie de Franklin* appeared in Paris, in which the French translator incorporated this passage on the year 1731, with acknowledgment to the *Décade*. It is pertinent to note that the publisher of this *Vie*, François Buisson, was also the publisher of a translation of Adam Smith's *Wealth of Nations* and other English and Scottish works. War, revolution, and dislike of the British government did not stop the French from a willingness to learn from the British.

The *Décade philosophique*, by its full title, addressed itself to literary and political as well as "philosophical" matters. The political had to be handled with care, but the "literary" made room for humor and imagination. Say contributed a good many pieces of this kind during the five years of his editorship. An example is a satire on bureaucracy, which had proliferated with the legal and administrative reforms introduced by the Revolution. Appearing in an early number of the *Décade*, it takes the form of a fictitious letter to the editors from an unknown correspondent, complaining of the paperwork necessary for a marriage. Say probably wrote it as a kind of filler, under pressure to produce something in print every "decade," or ten days, and it may reflect, with exaggeration, his experience with his own marriage a few months before. The word "septidi," in the following, is the name given to the seventh day of the "decade" in the new Revolutionary calendar. Two other words then new to the French language, but which became more permanent, may be found here: *bureaucratique* and *fonctionnaire*, the latter translated as "public servant."

BUREAUCRATIC MANNERS
Letter to the Editors of the *Décade*

It is said that the theater attacks vices that the laws cannot reach. Cannot the same be said of journals, especially such as yours, citizens, which always devotes a certain number of its pages to moral questions? I should think so, and think too that there are vices and absurdities that the theater can reach no better than the laws. Who then will render judgment, if not the journals? I urge you, citizens, to persist in the course you have adopted; the good that a respected periodical can do is immense. . . .

Have you not sometimes had business with public servants who abuse the need you have for them and the superiority over you given by their position, and so allow themselves to use words and actions toward you that they would never allow themselves if they had need of you? It is an abuse of this kind that I call to your attention. I need only tell you what has happened to me.

A friend of mine left Paris a short time ago to return to be married in the place he came from. He wrote to me a few days after his departure:

"My friend, I am desperate, angry at myself and my own stupidity. My marriage is about to be concluded; all difficulties are removed, everything is ready, but now has to be suspended. I have just been told that my marriage must be publicly announced in Paris, in the section where I used to live, *for three days!* It will take as long for my letter to reach you, and as long again for you to send me the needed papers—there is a whole mortal decade to wait! My future defies imagination; hurry to my old section, etc., etc."

I rushed to the municipality, and then to the section; I went to the police commissary and gave him the papers he needed; he gave me an appointment for the following septidi for his reply.

On the septidi (exactly the day for the mail to R . . . , where my friend is) I went to the police commissary before eleven o'clock. The necessary formality was a trifle; all that was needed was to certify the announcement, get the commissary's signature legalized, and put it all in the mail. I presented myself to him; he was fortunately alone, at his desk; I asked for the papers. He made a sign with his hand for me to be patient while he finished what he was doing. I walked about. Suddenly he rose, and began to rearrange his desk, or rather his table.

"That accursed girl," he said, referring to his servant. "She must displace my table every time she sweeps the floor." He pushed and pulled the table for more than a quarter of an hour until he had it just right, after which, noticing that there was no place for a chair between the table and the fireplace, he said, "Ho! ho! there must be a place for a person to sit down." He then began a new rearrangement, which seemed to me rather lengthy, for I felt that time was passing, and that if the papers did not go out by the next mail they would be delayed for several days. Still I said nothing to him, for he saw that I was there, and waiting. . . .

More complications followed, here omitted, concerning the appearance of the commissary's daughter-in-law who was looking for a lost pen, and then of the servant returning from the butcher shop with cuts of beef and mutton, which led to discussions of what they should have for dinner.

I thought I might have to stand by while they planned their dinner, and so went up to the commissary and said as gently as I could:

"Citizen commissary, let me say that I am pressed for time. If you could kindly—"

"Citizen, give me time. Must I leave everything else to attend to you? I have not lost a minute."

"I have been here an hour and a half," I answered, very politely.

"If you are so much in a hurry, go find someone else to give you satisfaction."

I was offended by his tone after waiting so long, and he began to sense how I felt despite my efforts to contain myself.

"Citizen," I said, "you well know that there is no one else to whom I can go. I only ask of you two lines and your signature."

"Well, sign it yourself," he said impatiently, tossing me his pen.

I then realized that it would have been better to leave him alone, that I had only added another snag to so many others, that being in danger of not getting my papers I should not have tried to prove to him that he was not doing his duty—that I had been wrong in being right. Finally, he relented, or, more exactly, he handed me my certificate with a scowl.

I left, very angry with this commissary, and while running to post my letter to my friend I kept saying to myself, under my breath: "In a Republic . . . to trifle with the time of a citizen! . . . these persons who are only employees of the people! . . . paid by the people!" But that my sufferings should not be lost for my fellow citizens. I promised myself to send the story of this encounter to you. I even flattered myself that this police commissary, who is not really a bad man, might even read it; and this is not impossible since I believe he goes for his little sip to the Café Procope, across from the old Comédie française, where they take your *Décade*. I wish him no harm, but I would not be sorry if he has a few reflections on the duties of public servants.

The theater offered other opportunities for serious reflection in a lighthearted vein. In January 1795, during the so-called Thermidorian reaction, Say reviewed a musical show then appearing at the Théâtre de la Cité. He enjoyed it, but took occasion to comment on the recent military victories of the Republic, on economics and the inflation that followed the recent abolition of price controls, and on the pursuit of "Jacobins" (who were thought to be known by their unpowdered hair) a few weeks after the Paris Jacobin club had been closed by the government.

While our fourteen armies dictate the terms of peace to all the powers of Europe and to our own internal rebels, it is amusing to see us squabbling among ourselves over a few musical productions and songs. It adds a new touch to the already too long chapter on human illogicalities. What some call a passing craze is good entertainment for others. This is all very well, but for the honor of the foremost Republic in the world let us not come to blows. Europe would have its revenge on us for a century of taking its fashions from us if we offer it the spectacle of civil war in a quarrel between purveyors of fashion. . . .

If it is true that the theater is a school we are sorry to see that it can give bad lessons. There are none contrary to morals in this bright little place, but there are some that are contrary to political economy, yes *political economy*, and nothing is indifferent in this matter, in which a single prejudice is harmful to the national prosperity. Here is the end of some verses that were *greatly applauded*:

> He who holds on to his money
> In our time of penury
> Robs both the worker and the state
> By his culpable economy.

The young people who wrote this play do not know that our troubles do not come from our paper money not showing itself. It shows itself all too much. Its superfluous circulation, caused by the enormous expenses of the government, is in part the cause of the very high price of all necessary goods. These necessary goods exist in no greater quantity than in the past; it is the sign that represents them that has tripled. The more the government or private persons put these signs into circulation, the more they fall in value. What we need is more goods in circulation, not more paper money. The more that necessities are purchased, the more those who need them are deprived. It is therefore false to say that whoever holds on to his money *robs the worker and the state*. And, in another place, that *we need more buyers, not more hands*.

Another error in the piece, related to this one, is that a display of luxury is needed to give life to trade. It would take too much detail to demonstrate that luxurious display comes only with the sacrifice of what is useful, and is always the neighbor of poverty; that true luxury, luxury as best understood, consists in the abundance of necessary goods, the good quality of what is consumed, and the convenience and cleanness of whatever we touch.

We have been sorry too to hear declarations against unpowdered hair. It is a great mistake to suppose that headdress is a sure indication of opinions. If there were to be only one style of headdress we should perhaps choose the one that disguises least, spoils nature least, and is also the most good-looking, favored by artists and philosophers, and preferred by Pericles and Virgil, who were no Jacobins. It is possible to have a very clean head without powder, and in fact hard to keep it clean with powder and pomade. No doubt greasy hair is ugly, but a head full of flour is not pretty. In any case, if you want to detect a Jacobin by this test you will be very mistaken. You can be sure that nowadays there is no Jacobin without well tended hair.

In the spring of 1796 Say's colleague at the *Décade philosophique*, Amaury Duval, proposed what he called a "theater of the people" as a means of raising the moral and intellectual level of the general population. Say disagreed, and put his disagreement in a message "from Boniface Véridick to Polyscope," a literary device that he used occasionally in the *Décade*, in which Say as Véridick, the "truth teller," conveyed his thoughts to Polyscope, the "many-seeing," who was Amaury Duval. The message turned into a six-page disquisition on education and the arts, with sarcastic references to the old French nobility and the ancient Greeks and Romans, and concluding with a description of what Say thought would be a perfect society. It would be a society in which the good life for most people would come from their own productivity in their own daily occupations.

Alas, my dear Polyscope, I cannot share your opinion. . . .

You say, dear Polyscope, that it is not enough to have schools for children, that we need them for those *grown-up children* who by fortune or circumstance have been unable to learn the principles of morality and politics. Let us distinguish; let us clarify our ideas. There are of course many ignorant persons, and many whose education has been neglected. Three-quarters of the inhabitants of our so-called civilized country cannot read or write. I agree; but what instruction do they need? They need an instruction, it seems to me, that makes them more capable in their occupation, whatever it may be. The more they produce, and the more they improve their product, the more they will be at ease in their families and the more the country will be enriched by their labors. And where will they learn this? In their own setting, if they are assiduous and hard-working, and not at all at the theater. They must know also how to write and count so as to keep order in their small affairs, and to know when necessary how to write a letter or draw up a report. Certainly the theater will teach them none of these things. . . .

What then are theaters good for? To spread good taste in literature and the arts, and to refine our way of living. We should have theaters as we have painters and makers of statuary, to beautify our country and enlarge the imagination of its inhabitants. We should encourage them to provide us with objects worthy of the majesty of a great people, objects that induce love of the laws and of one's country. In that, my dear Polyscope, we are in agreement; but let not our government be director of a troop of actors, and let there be no national theaters or *theater for the people*.

Classical republicanism with its civic virtue, vast spectacles, and imposing monuments, was all very well, but we moderns can do better.

Popular spectacles and circuses were good for the ancients, among whom a numerous class of unemployed citizens, especially in the cities, were contemptuous of the useful arts, and when unarmed could do nothing but form cabals in public places, consume the freely distributed grain brought from conquered provinces, and parade their idleness in festivals given by magistrates eager to capture their favor. Such people were true nobles, in beggarly circumstances to be sure, but still nobles; and the slaves, the working class of their society, formed the Third Estate. It should be very different with us. Let us give up the desire and hope of making our fellow citizens into a people of Greeks and Romans. We can do much better than that. Our modern customs, our northerly location, the great size of our states almost equal in civilization, together with the relations between them, the invention of paper and printing, our progress in the sciences, navigation, commerce and the postal service, all make it our law to avoid servile copying of the ancients, to be ourselves, to attain the only degree of improvement and happiness of which we are capable.

Here is how I imagine a condition of improvement and happiness in a great modern state such as France. I should wish first of all that it be at peace and that its citizens be united in a general good will and mutual trust. I should wish for a firm government to guarantee its independence abroad and security at home. I should wish its agriculture and many kinds of industry to be brilliantly active, and for abundance to be evident in its seaports filled with ships, its canals and rivers covered with boats, and its markets clean and well supplied. I should wish that every rural worker and every town artisan might have, if not an independent property, at least the prospect of obtaining one for his old age, if only in the form of a small lifetime annuity. I should wish that every household should show signs of ease, but not opulence, in possessing clean and well-kept utensils, garments of good cloth, and white linen; and that everyone should know how to read and have a few books in his closet for instruction on the practical arts, as well as a few newspapers to inform him on the interests of his country. I should wish that the visitors to our public establishments should feel, not the sadness aroused by the sight of suffering humanity [as by seeing crucifixes in churches?] but the contentment inspired by the sight of humanity relieved. I should wish, in a word, that in a great republic there should be not a single idler whose unproductive existence would be a burden to society, and not one poor person to complain that, by his work and good conduct, he cannot earn an easy subsistence or lead a life that the English would call "comfortable."

At this point Say has a long footnote recommending adoption of the word "comfortable" in French, and elaborating on its meaning. "Comfort" had in fact entered the English language from the Norman French of the twelfth century, and would reenter French only in the nineteenth.

This word, which we should adopt because it evokes an idea that we can express only in paraphrase, means that a person has an inner sense of easiness, contentment and convenience. A house is comfortable when it has a convenient distribution of space, a favorable location, and a pleasant view; when its doors, windows and fireplaces are well built, but without luxury; when everything is within reach, and in short when one is neither burdened by superfluities nor in need of necessities. Everything we use can be either comfortable or not. Clothing is comfortable when it allows fresh air to reach our body in the heat of summer and envelops it easily in winter. After a long day's effort when we feel the need of restoring our strength a solid dinner and a glass of good wine are comfortable. My friends, put this word in your dictionary, and may you enjoy all it expresses!

Say became more free to comment on more serious matters as the Terror receded and the emergency government was dismantled. In 1795 the French armies passed from the defensive to the offensive and occupied the Netherlands and the German Rhineland. The kings of Prussia and Spain made peace with the revolutionary Republic. Only Austria and Great Britain remained at war with France. The National Convention, having thus broken up the alliance against it, and after repressing two armed invasions of its hall in the spring of 1795, appointed a committee on the constitution, commonly known as the Committee of Eleven. The committee soon decided that the constitution adopted in 1793, which had been suspended for the duration of the war, should not be put into effect. It proposed a wholly new constitution, to be preceded by a declaration of rights and going on to more than three hundred articles. These featured, among much else, a division of powers in which an Executive Directory was to be elected by a legislative body, itself divided into a lower chamber to be called the Council of Five Hundred and an upper chamber called the Council of Elders (the *Anciens*, or men who had to be at least forty years old).

For the *Décade* of 20 Messidor of the Year III (July 8, 1795) Say wrote a critique of this proposal:

> . . . The constitution proposed by the Committee of Eleven presents in general a firm government, capable of repressing excesses and not likely to fall into excesses itself. But isn't it too complicated? Doesn't it embrace matters that go beyond a simple *division of powers*? For that is what we should understand by the word *Constitution*.
>
> It is said that the great art in governing is not to govern too much. A law is a constraint; a fundamental law is a constraint on the governed as well as on the government. A constitutional code, if complicated, and so more often touching on the passions and prejudices of individu-

als, will be the more often attacked and the more easily subverted. So to have few constitutional laws is not only an advantage to the people but an assurance of the durability of the constitutional laws themselves.

It is hence desirable to limit a constitution to the establishment of a government, and for it to contain no laws that can be more appropriately enacted by the government itself. If we are so careful to provide a future government with laws already made we seem to suppose in advance that it may be unable to do any good, or that it can betray the state. The proposed constitution begins with a Declaration of Rights. Let us not be too impressed by the words Declaration of Rights, or by the precedent of all the constitutions proposed, adopted and violated since the beginning of the Revolution; let us see whether it is advisable to place such a declaration, establishing rights in their fullest extent, at the head of a constitution that must necessarily restrict them. The declaration states that *law is the expression of the general will*, but the constitution provides that law is simply the will of the Council of Five Hundred and the Council of Elders. Note also that some of its articles are only maxims, such as that *The aim of society is the general happiness*. Others are duties: *Any citizen summoned or seized by authority of the law should obey instantly*.

It is then not too hazardous to say that a declaration of rights, very useful at the time of the revolution, when the need was to establish principles by which the former government would be discredited in public opinion, is superfluous, to say the least, now that these rights are recognized; and that to proclaim others is unnecessary.

It will perhaps be said that a usurper would be stopped by such a declaration, but Robespierre himself said, in speaking to the Jacobin club, *People, you are betrayed; take back to yourselves the exercise of your sovereignty!*

It might be enough, as an introduction or stated reason for the constitution, to give it simply this preamble: *The French people, to assure for all individuals who compose it tranquillity, security of person and property, and the liberty compatible with life in a large society, has ordained the organization of its government as follows*. That is our *Arma virumque cano*. It was not necessary to bring in the Supreme Being as witness to the affair. The constitution is not an oath; it is a contract founded on the interest of the contracting parties, and revocable at their will.

At this point the reader may be reminded of the preamble to the federal Constitution of the United States, in which "we the people" hope to assure domestic tranquillity and ordain a new form of government. There is no reason, however, to suppose that Say had any such resemblance in mind; the French in 1795 were too preoccupied with their own affairs to be much aware of what had recently happened in America. There is another curious resemblance of generally opposite tenor, anticipating the French constitution of the Year VIII, enacted at the end of 1799 after Bonaparte's coup d'état. By this arrangement the legislative procedure after 1799 was conducted in two chambers, a Tribunate and a Legislative Body. The Tribunate (of which Say would become a member) debated and sent proposed laws to the Legislative Body, which without debate either rejected or enacted them after hearing the arguments of spokesmen for the Tribunate and for the executive power. Bonaparte's Legislative Body engaged in no debate itself; it merely judged, and enacted if it approved. Say favored a similar provision (unsuccessfully) for what became the constitution under the Directory. He thought that the Council of Elders should listen in silence.

It is a good idea in this project to leave the definitive decision to a body of Elders, in which no proposal can originate. This body will thus not support a proposal simply because it is *its own*, and its judgment will be the more equitable. Should we not make it even more impassive? We need only forbid it the power of discussion. None of its members having announced his opinion in open debate, none would have his self-esteem involved in the deliberation; each one's mind would be open to the truth whenever it presented itself. Vanity, which makes men do so many foolish things, would be involved only in issuing good decrees. But in that case the Council of Elders would have to hear some debates. . . .

Say next launches into a long discussion of the meaning of executive, legislative, and judicial powers, their separation in principle and unavoidable overlap in practice. He then takes up the question, on the minds of many in 1795, of how to avoid such "troubles" as those of preceding years. He fears that provisions in the proposed constitution may not be enough, and indeed they were to prove inadequate in the political crisis of 1799. He foresees some such takeover of power as was to be effected by Bonaparte. To prevent it, he proposes a legalized temporary dictatorship such as that of the Committee of Public Safety of 1793–94.

The Committee of Eleven has foreseen that troubles may arise in the Republic that necessitate the renewal of the legislature or its removal to another place; and it has stipulated the procedure for such a removal or renewal. But should we not fear that such precautions may be useless, or even harmful? When a government is attacked it should not be reduced to either flight or dissolution; we would then fall back into the perpetual circle of insurrections. It must be remembered that a government divided among many hands may be excellent in ordinary times, but in times of division it would tear itself to pieces, and anarchy would ensue. Whoever has given thought to recent events and to the history of republics will be convinced that there is only one way to save the state in perilous circumstances. It is to draw together all the powers and energy of government into a few hands worthy of confidence. Otherwise there is no unity and no force. It seems then that the constitution should do no more than assign to the Council of Elders the power to appoint, for a fixed length of time, a Committee of Public Safety, as soon as it believes the country to be in danger [*la patrie en danger*, the cry raised when France was invaded in 1792].

And abruptly changing the subject:

One malady to which political bodies are liable is the excessive accumulation of laws. Their number soon prevents the citizen from knowing what they are; and hence the need for lawyers. Some laws soon provide the means for eluding others; and hence comes chicanery. A way to avoid this disadvantage might be to create a body or a committee whose function would be a continuing review of all decrees, to compare and classify them, and propose to the legislative body the suppression or rewording needed to simplify the system of legislation. . . .

And in conclusion, a somewhat doubtful expression of the hope that the years of revolution may be followed by a long period of stability and peaceable satisfaction:

We know from experience that for a constitution to be maintained it is not enough for it to be decreed, adopted, and sworn to. It must also be so suited to the men and circumstances for which it is made that no need of changing it is even felt. What it prescribes must appear to be so easy and natural that it is accepted by habit, for it is habit alone that attaches most people to institutions. If these conditions are not met, the new constitution, far from ending the convulsions that we have sadly experienced, would on the contrary become the source of new convulsions whose end we cannot foresee without a shudder.

Say's advice as published in the *Décade* had no effect. The project submitted by the Committee of Eleven was adopted virtually without change. Contrary to what Say would prefer, it began with an invocation of the Supreme Being, proclaimed a declaration of rights (supplemented by a declaration of duties), and running to 377 articles was longer and more complicated than the preceding constitutions of 1791 and 1793. It reflected none of Say's distaste for talkative and irresponsible legislative bodies. Its Council of Elders would debate and not merely listen.

The constitution of 1795 and ensuing Directory have been called less "democratic" and more "bourgeois" than the regime of 1793 and abortive constitution of that year. It is true that they diluted the popular vote through a system of electoral colleges, and they made no mention, as in 1793, of rights to popular insurrection, steady employment, poor relief, and universal education at public expense.

But Say was less "reactionary" than many republicans under the Directory. Like them, he feared popular turbulence, but he did not fulminate against Jacobins or dwell in righteous horror on what had happened during the Terror, which he saw as a consequence of revolutionary circumstances in time of war. He could think Robespierre a usurper because, in his view, Robespierre had usurped the powers not of the monarchy but of the National Convention and its Committee of Public Safety. He could strike a conservative note when he said, like Edmund Burke, that a durable constitution must rest upon habit. But his main difference from most republicans, and indeed from Burke, was that he had less faith in forms of law and government, and expected a better world of the future to come from economic activity.

This interest in economic development was expressed in a long article in the *Décade* in November 1798 on the Conservatoire des Arts et Métiers. This institution, in which Say would be a "pupil" for a short time in 1804 and its professor of political economy beginning in 1821, was a creation of the Revolution, but like others it built on similar efforts made during the Old Regime. Its name raises difficulties of translation. A *métier* was a craft or trade. An *art* was a training or skill used for a productive purpose, and although this meaning also exists in English it has a wider scope in French, where it can refer to any practical application of knowledge, so that *les arts* is sometimes best translated as "practical arts." An *artiste*, therefore, may be a painter or musician, but he or she may also be a weaver, an embroiderer, a building contractor, or an inventor. The word *machine*, when it occurs in the following passage, may mean (as in English at that time) any ingenious mechanical contrivance rather than a machine in a later sense.

Three-quarters of Say's article, which ran to twelve pages in the *Décade*, is a quotation from a speech by Henri Grégoire. This remarkable man, a Catholic priest, was one of the liberal Catholics who accepted the Revolution in its successive phases, became a bishop in the reorganized church, took the lead in extending equal civil rights to Jews and free blacks, urged the abolition of slavery in the colonies, and had a long life until 1831 during which he wrote many books, including one arguing that blacks had potentially the same aptitudes and abilities as whites, which was not well received in the United States. In 1798 Say quoted the speech in which Grégoire supported the Conservatory of Arts and Trades (as we shall call it), by using economic arguments that Say could applaud.

Say began, in his own words:

Among the institutions created by the Revolution as a basis of public prosperity will unquestionably be the Conservatory of Arts and Trades. Readers may appreciate our tracing the origin, progress, aim, and advantages of this fine establishment, with which the government is now occupying itself, and which only awaits the first signs of a general peace to enjoy an outstanding reputation.

The famous Vaucanson, in his passion for the useful arts to which he contributed with such success, conceived a project for bringing together the machines that he had invented, and for this purpose he bought a house in the rue de Charonne which still today serves as a depository.

At the time of his death in 1782 he bequeathed to the government the machines and tools that existed in his workshops. There were more than sixty models deserving to be known to the public.

In 1783 the controller-general, Joly de Fleury, appointed Vandermonde, a member of the Academy of Sciences, to make plans for the preservation of Vaucanson's precious legacy, as well as machines and models subsequently invented, which were to be donated by their creators on receiving national awards.

This collection grew rapidly with the discoveries and productions of our artists. In 1784 the depository was definitively fixed in the rue de Charonne when the government purchased Vaucanson's house.

Early in the Revolution the Constituent Assembly acted to give new encouragements to the Arts and Trades. It voted an annual sum of 300,000 livres to be distributed to artists as awards for their works or researches, to be judged by a jury instituted for this purpose, called the Bureau of Consultation on Arts and Trades.

To encourage the Arts it was not enough to make awards; it was thought necessary also to assure inventors of the peaceable enjoyment of the fruits of their genius. In 1791 the Assembly recognized this truly sacred property right, and placed it under special protection of the law by establishing *patents of invention.*

By this law those who wish to profit from this legal guarantee are required to transmit models to the government, as well as drawings and exact descriptions of their procedure. Secrecy is faithfully guarded, but on expiration of the patent the discovery is no longer the property of its author but becomes that of the public.

On January 1, 1792, the total expenditure on the depository for Vaucanson's machines, over a period of nine years, was no more than

60,000 livres, and the collection during these years had grown to 300 machines, among which are looms, machines for carding and spinning cotton, stocking-frames, and machines for producing boot-laces, braids, ribbons, and many other such things of an extreme importance for our manufactures.

Say gives a vivid account of the vandalism that accompanied the insurrection of August 1792, but stresses the continuing care for such valuable objects taken by successive governments of the Revolution.

In August 1792 some men in a blind fury destroyed several monuments of the Arts. They found signs of feudalism in simple architectural decorations, and broke them up. They saw the effigy of a king in a statue of a god, and tore it down. They burned paintings by Titian and Leonardo da Vinci in which some of the figures wore crowns. The bust of Linnaeus was mutilated in the Jardin des Plantes, where it stood among the varied products of Nature that he had described and classified. These excesses, which the ignorance of their perpetrators can explain but not justify, were finally stopped by the Legislative Assembly, which hastened to set up a Commission on Monuments, which it charged with identifying objects worthy of preservation for the glory of the Arts, and with separating out everything related to the Sciences and Trades in the immense inheritance then coming to the nation at this time.

This commission showed too little zeal or activity in the functions confided to it, and was suppressed in Frimaire of the Year II [December 1793] and replaced by a Temporary Commission on the Arts.

The members of this commission justified the confidence of the Committee on Public Instruction which had appointed them. They took all parts of the Sciences as their domain, but they gave particular attention to finding what could be useful to the Arts and Trades, and they succeeded after great efforts in preserving for the Republic over 800 objects in the mechanical arts essential to progress in agriculture and manufactures.

This priceless collection was placed in a building in the rue de l'Université. But it remained useless for Artists since defects in the site made it impossible to admit them.

France also already possessed another large quantity of industrial riches hitherto lost to the Arts. The former Academy of Sciences [abolished in 1793, restored as a "class" within the National Institute in 1795] had built up over more than a century a cabinet containing many valuable models, both for the history of the arts and the progress of industry. These models also will find a place in the new Conservatory. Though it might seem incredible, for the first time in a hundred years the public will be able to view the master-works of invention produced by French practitioners of the practical arts.

The committees on Public Instruction and on Agriculture, after ascertaining the number and importance of machines and instruments assembled by the Temporary Commission, obtained from the Convention in Vendémiaire of the Year III [October 1794] the creation of a *Conservatory of Arts*, composed of three demonstrators and a draftsman. Obstacles arising mainly from the difficult circumstances of that time led to neglect of this commendable institution. The Council of Five Hundred was even surprised into passing a resolution to suppress it, but this resolution provoked in the Council of Elders an excellent report by Citizen Alquier, so that the resolution was rejected and the Conservatory maintained. The Five Hundred took up the subject again, and the estimable Grégoire prepared a report containing so many useful views and interesting facts that we quote a large part of it here.

We select here only a small portion of Grégoire's speech as reproduced by Say. It is the part that expresses important ideas in economics, at a time when the industrial revolution was beginning in France as well as England, though at a slower pace, and when it was feared that new inventions would throw many out of work. We put Grégoire's words in quotation marks as Say did.

"It is surprising to hear people still claim that the improvement of industry and simplification of labor are dangerous because, they say, they deprive many workers of the means of making a living. It was thus that the copyists of manuscripts argued when printing was invented, and that the boatmen of London reasoned, even threatening violent action, when the Westminster bridge was built; and only seven years ago at Le Havre and Rouen machines for spinning cotton had to be hidden. The consequence of this puerile objection would be our having to break up our stocking-frames, our machines for twisting silk threads and other valuable innovations produced by industry for the good of society. It takes no great effort of reflection to realize that we obtain more products for a given input of labor, that when labor is simplified the price paid for labor is reduced, and that if workers must give the products of their art at a lower [unit] price they produce them in greater quantity, and also pay less for goods they need for their own use; and finally, that this is the only way to establish a lucrative trade and meet the competition of foreign industry. When a machine is invented that saves time and effort there are in the long run no fewer hands employed, but more objects are produced; the conveniences of life are more widespread and come within the means of persons of modest income. Two hundred years ago only the rich could wear stockings.

Now if we had a machine for making shoes no one would go barefoot. The invention of printing has not diminished the number of those who work on multiplying the copies of books; there are now more printers than there used to be copyists. And the effect of this invention has been to multiply the means of reading and education, so that the poorest person can now possess at least an almanac. . . ."

Grégoire continues, having in mind the recent French victories in a war not yet terminated:

"But supposing that a nation has won a superiority that frees it from a foreign yoke, this advantage will soon be lost unless it takes effective measures to advance the Arts to a greater perfection, and to spread more widely the new processes and instruments.

"The Conservatory of Arts and Trades is an establishment well suited to this end.

"The Arts and Trades are taught elsewhere, in workshops, and the chemical aspect is also not taught in the Conservatory. What will be learned there is recent improvements in procedures, the most effective construction of machines and tools, their combination of movements and employment of forces. This part of the sciences is both new and useful. This teaching, alongside actual models, is not at all abstractly systematic; it is based only on experience. And in addition to the machines there will be:

1. Samples of the products of national and foreign manufacturers, for purposes of comparison.
2. The design of each machine.
3. A description that so to speak preserves the thought of the inventor. . . .

"People often bother the government with pretended secrets and pretended discoveries. I am not speaking of those who without the least idea of friction come to give us a demonstration of perpetual motion. Others propose ideas that are indeed sound, but have already been realized. It will be enough in the future to send them to the Conservatory. There they will be told: your art has already reached this point; see what you can add to its progress. Thus the nation will not pay several times for the same thing. The disconcerted charlatan and imitator will no longer invade the funds intended for awards to which only the inventor has a right. . . ."

After much else by Grégoire, here omitted, Say resumes and concludes:

These arguments advanced by Citizen Grégoire persuaded the two Councils, in the month of Floréal last, to enact a law dedicating a part of the former priory of Saint-Martin, in the street of that name, to the *Conservatory of Arts and Trades*. Delays due to certain formalities will put off until next spring the time when the people can have full enjoyment of this establishment, in which the instruments, machines, and all kinds of processes and products of human industry will be displayed, classified, and explained.

There the objects scattered in the depositories we have noted will be brought together. They will be open provisionally to all interested persons, and will be augmented from day to day by other objects that artists honor themselves by sending in. A correspondence relative to the Arts has already begun, among both French and foreign artists.

In addition to work on repairing machines the Conservatory is now busy with classifying the instruments and sample products of industry. It is working also on preparing the exhibition halls, and on:

1. The formation of a library of technical books.
2. The manufacture of sewing needles. Although there is already a factory for this purpose at Aix-la-Chapelle it has been thought that, for the instruction of artisans, a similar workshop should be set up in Paris for processes for the simplification of labor and the improvement of needles. An iron oxide grindstone invented by Citizen Molard will be used there.
3. The construction of a steam engine to impart movement to various mechanical assemblages.
4. The economical fabrication of paper cylinders, already successfully employed for the finishing of fabrics, and which should be used more widely. For this purpose the Government has designated song books and other works for recycling. . . .

It cannot be doubted that such powerful encouragements, together with the honors awarded each year to persons distinguishing themselves in the mechanical arts, will produce in the future the most favorable effects for French industry.

It is amusing to see the steam engine so casually mentioned between the sewing needles and the paper cylinders. The nineteenth century would be the age of steam. But it may be that even in England, where the stationary steam engine was already widely used, not many would have given it more attention in 1798 in a similar context. Say saw its importance when he reported on a visit to England sixteen years later.

Chapter Two

THE SOBER UTOPIAN

THE FIRST PIECE of writing by Jean-Baptiste Say to be published in book form was his *Olbia*, or *Olbie* in French, a word which he tells us he took from the Greek *olbios*, meaning the happiness that comes from a proper enjoyment of wealth. A little book of 132 pages, published in 1800, it is a transitional work, anticipating some of the thoughts in his *Treatise on Political Economy* of 1803, and reflecting his association since 1794 with the *Décade philosophique*, with members of the newly founded National Institute, and with the *Idéologues* who at first welcomed the takeover of the government by General Napoleon Bonaparte in 1799.

Olbia originated as a paper submitted in a prize contest set up by the Class in Moral and Political Science of the Institute. Of the six sections of this Class, one was devoted to Political Economy, by that name. With science understood as any body of knowledge based on careful observation, political economy was classified as a moral science because, unlike the natural sciences, it took account of human will, decision, and action, both individual and collective, and so with the happiness or misery of which human beings were capable.

The prize offered was to go for the best paper in answer to the question: "What are the means of establishing moral behavior among a people?" As it happened, the prize was never awarded, although the most famous of the *idéologues* and member of the Institute, Destutt de Tracy, was among the contestants. Say's *Olbia* was in fact a strange contribution to a learned society. It was in effect a utopia, though the word "utopia" occurs nowhere except in a passing reference to some of the more bizarre ideas in the famous *Utopia* of Thomas More. In rejecting Say's work the prize committee explained to him that it contained only pictures or *tableaux*, but no systematic treatment of the question asked. Say replied to this objection in a short introduction when he published his *Olbia*. He had supposed, he said, that the Institute had wished to elicit writings that would "disseminate useful truths and destroy dangerous errors."

Now it is not by abstractions that one achieves this purpose. It is, unless I am mistaken, by clothing the precepts of reason with the graces of eloquence and the charms of feeling. Doubtless I am far from achieving this goal, but should the committee of the Institute blame me for having tried?

Since my principal aim in writing this work was to make myself useful, I have thought I should print it. And what time was ever more favorable for publishing a work on the moral behavior of a nation than the time we are now in? Men whose outstanding talents and moral worth are uncontested even by their greatest enemies have adopted a plan [the Consulate under Bonaparte] to stabilize the Republic by observing the rules of moral science, and have been put by their fellow citizens into the highest public offices. Surely it is a time when we can allow ourselves the dreams of a philanthropic imagination. I only regret having to keep within the bounds of an academic discourse a work which, by the importance of its subject and possibilities for further development, would provide material for a whole book.

Say was himself among those talented and moral individuals now put into public office. He became a member of the Tribunate, a branch of the legislative apparatus created by the constitution of the Year VIII, and on the title page of his *Olbia*, after his name, he proudly added *Membre du Tribunat*.

For so small a book, *Olbia* is ungainly and ill-proportioned. It is loaded with footnotes and endnotes. It begins crisply, but fails even to mention Olbia until page 20, and at the end trails off into quotation of fourteen wise sayings by famous authors from Plutarch through Francis Bacon, La Fontaine, and Voltaire, to conclude with six maxims by Benjamin Franklin's Poor Richard. Then come the more than twenty endnotes, occupying more than the final third of the small volume. Yet the book is a utopia of the kind that an economist might write; its emphasis is on production, efficiency, and a well-understood self-interest. It is also a moral tract, showing how in France, as in Adam Smith's Scotland and later in the United States, political economy emerged as a specialty within moral philosophy.

The book begins with a series of definitions concerning the words *moeurs*, *morale*, and *moralité*. Their definition requires some comments on translation. The word *moeurs* has always been difficult to render in English; it is often translated as "manners" or "manners and customs," with a general meaning of what would now be called culture. In Say's usage it seems best to translate it as "moral behavior," meaning not necessarily good behavior but a behavior that may be either good or bad. For *la morale* it is often best to call it the theory, knowledge, or science of morality, or of value judgments concerning good and bad. For *moralité* we can usually make do with "morality." In this semantic connection the reader may be reminded that the word *science* means any sound knowledge based on observation, as in the "science" of Poor Richard. The word *nation*, in the following pages, is without the ethnic content that it acquired in the nineteenth and twentieth centuries; its meaning is civic and political, referring to a people or society living under a government. And *l'homme*, like "man" in English, often refers to all human beings without regard to age or sex.

Here are the opening words of *Olbia*:

By moral behavior (*les moeurs*), applied to humans, we must understand not only the honest and regular relations between the two sexes but the constant habits of a person or nation in what concerns the conduct of life.

Moral science is the science of moral behavior. (*La morale est la science des moeurs.*) I say "science" because, in the social state, the rules of conduct are not all given by nature; they are learned. It is true that they are learned from childhood and by routine; but is not language, which is also a science, also learned in the same way?

Morality (*la moralité*) is the habit of consulting the rules of moral science (*la morale*) in all one's actions. Among all beings, man alone seems capable of possessing this admirable faculty.

The aim of moral science is to obtain for men all the happiness compatible with their nature. . . .

The author then launches into a discussion of education, which he finds has two parts, one for instilling good moral and physical habits, and the other for "instruction," meaning the conveyance of knowledge. Rousseau thought the former more important, and it is indeed important, but:

Yet however important this part of education may be, it would be a great mistake to think that the part relating to instruction is of no importance for moral science. Instruction has two great advantages for moral behavior: first, it softens such behavior; and, second, it enlightens us on our true interests.

The softening effect of instruction is to turn our ideas toward innocent and useful objects. Well-instructed men, in general, do less harm or damage than those who lack instruction. Those who study agriculture, those who know what pains it takes to make a plant grow or raise a tree and who understand their economic uses, are less likely to destroy them than ignorant persons who have no idea of the value of these products. Similarly, those who have studied the bases on which the social order and happiness are founded will never wantonly undermine them.

But it is mainly in enlightening us on our true interests that instruction is helpful to moral science. The worker who drinks up a week's income in a few hours, who goes home drunk, beats his wife, and corrupts by his example the children who might become the support of his old age, and who in the end ruins his health and dies in the poorhouse, makes a worse calculation than the diligent worker who instead of wasting accumulates his small savings, with the interest upon them, and provides for an old age which he passes in the bosom of an active family that he has made happy, and by which he is adored.

It is especially important in a free State for the people to be enlightened. It is from the people that lawful power arises, and from the summit of such power that either virtue or corruption then flow down. The men in high office are responsible for all appointments, all institutions, and the force of their example. If they are inept, evil minded, and corrupt, ineptitude, perversity, and corruption will inundate the whole social pyramid. . . .

Clearly Say relies on the enlightened action of an educated elite. But not on that alone; the poorest classes must also be brought to understand their own need for education, and specifically for "instruction."

A nation that has bad moral behavior but good books should do all it can for the teaching of reading.

The poor man, assailed by his own needs, sees in black signs on white paper only a learned futility. He is unaware that the highest knowledge, such as the useful ideas of political economy, the fertile sources of the happiness of nations, are concealed in these characters that he scorns, and that if his forefathers had been able to lift the veil he himself would not be reduced to sharing a piece of black bread with his rude family in a hut fit for savages.

Do you wish such a man to provide instruction for his children? Then begin by giving him enough tranquillity and an adequate share of well-being for him to be able to think of something that will always be of secondary usefulness in his eyes.

This adequate share of well-being can only result from a well-ordered share in the general wealth, which itself can only be the fruit of a good system of political economy, an important science, the most important of all if the morality and happiness of men are to be thought worthy of their study.

At this point Say inserts one of his footnotes, on the importance of the kind of book on which he would soon begin to work and would publish three years later.

Whoever would write an elementary treatise on Political Economy, suitable to be taught in the public schools and to be understood by lower-level public officials, as well as by country people and artisans, would be a great benefactor to his country.

The main text continues:

> It is vain to try to force the speed at which natural events happen. Good education and instruction, which have modest comfort as their source and good moral behavior as their consequence, will never germinate except in easy circumstances for the people. That is what must come first. If we refuse to begin at the beginning we shall create institutions in name only, which may indeed appear to be solid and impressive, but would soon be like those festoons of foliage and artificial trees cut in the woods to embellish a festival, superb vegetables without roots that imitate rural nature for a while, but being unable to bear flowers or fruits soon become only a pompous arrangement of desiccated wood. . . .
>
> We want men to conduct themselves well. Is it enough to command them? Our first teacher, experience, tells us that it is not. If the best precepts, supported by the authority of laws, use of force, and divine sanction, were enough to make men virtuous there would be no nation that was not a model of all the virtues; for there is no nation whose laws do not so command, and no religion that does not threaten the sinner with frightful punishments or promise magnificent rewards for right living. But look at these well-indoctrinated nations. Is there a single one where the ambitious man has not crushed his rivals, or vengeance exercised its furies, or the love of lucre not inspired the most shameful cheating and vilest prostitutions?

Here the author refers to one of his endnotes, the longest of all, where in fourteen pages he denounces all organized religions in language that would be excessive even for Voltaire, but which in the 1790s even mild revolutionaries and moderate republicans could sometimes use. He goes on:

> It is said that virtue should be made loveable. I would dare to add that it should be made profitable. Vice is ugly; let us also make it ruinous.

To illustrate this point, after a few words on Lycurgus and Sparta, he chooses a more recent and relevant example. It is obviously the United States, which he praises in terms that Americans would not find altogether flattering.

> In some modern colonies that have established their institutions on these principles they have been crowned with success. Most of the Europeans who settled on the coasts of North America left behind them neither the regrets nor the esteem of their former countrymen. Some were insolvent or even fraudulent debtors, and some were even worse.

Arrived on the new continent, they had to respect among themselves the only qualities that could preserve their newly born society. Employment, power, credit, and fortune went to those known for their reliability, good conduct, and love of work. Men without probity in their affairs, without decency towards women, without good will towards their brothers, could not subsist. They had to change character, or depart. So the moral behavior of this people, in general, has provided the nations of Europe even during the storms of revolution with examples of virtues unknown to the Europeans. The rejects of these nations have deservedly become their model.

After this brief encomium, Say gets to the point of describing the imaginary country of Olbia. It is a country that has undergone a revolution some fifty years before, and so is not hampered by the bad habits of its old regime.

I will now show these same principles put into practice in a society that has established its liberty on the ruins of an absolute monarchy, and has consolidated its edifice of liberty by a total change in its moral behavior, or, if you like, its habits. This people, which lives in a country called Olbia, after enjoying a liberty founded on good laws for half a century, is too advanced in the way of right thinking to be any longer embarrassed by a memory of its former depravities. They are embarrassed only by faults that they are still capable of committing.

I shall take only a few examples from the Olbians. They are all that my present limits allow me. But they are enough, I hope, to stimulate broader and more coordinated and perhaps more correct ideas, so that my work though imperfect will not be useless. . . .

It will be seen that I assume that the leaders of the nation, on whom its institutions depend, have a firm will to regenerate the moral habits of their fellow citizens; otherwise it would be superfluous to consider the matter.

Here we must understand that Say, so far as he was thinking of the application of his fable to the real world at all, was thinking of Bonaparte and the numerous intellectuals and other civilians who favored Bonaparte's coup d'état and the new constitution of the Year VIII in these early months of the Consulate. Say reinforces this point in a footnote:

. . . a revolution in political institutions has never been consolidated unless there has been at the same time a revolution in its moral habits. It is true that the former revolution makes the latter easy. To reform the moral behavior of a people, we have a fine institution in the Republic.

And the main text:

. . . The legislators of nations, and the most influential of their magistrates, orators and writers, should work with me in this enterprise. I call on my fellow citizens who can have an influence on the national moral behavior, those in high office and those of talents, to devote themselves to the accomplishment of this great and laudable work. Let them realize how much solid glory will result for themselves, and how much true happiness for all!

After this exhortation to his compatriots actually living in France, the author at last begins to describe life in Olbia. He does so in the past tense, as if just returning from a visit there and recounting its history. He has found a country where a "real" equality prevails, though only relatively, since there are still people who do not have to work for a living. In the following pages the French *aisance* is translated as "comfort." Say had said in the *Décade philosophique* in 1796 that this English word should be taken into French, and would say so again in his *Treatise*.

After the revolution that let the Olbians conduct themselves by the counsels of reason rather than by their former ways the leading men of the nation took steps to reduce the too great inequality of fortunes. They knew that, to form good moral behavior, the most favorable situation is one where most families composing the nation live in an honest comfort, and where excessive opulence is as rare as extreme indigence.

Poverty exposes to continual temptations, and indeed to imperative needs. . . .

Great wealth is no less damaging to good moral behavior. . . .

But it is not by regulations and sumptuary laws that a nation is preserved from opulence and poverty. It is by a complete system of legislation and administration. Hence the primary book on moral science for the Olbians was a good Treatise on Political Economy. They established a kind of academy to be the depository of this book. Any citizen wishing to fill a position through appointment by the highest magistrates had to subject himself to a public questioning on the principles of this science, which he could attack or defend as he chose. His mere knowledge of them was enough for the Academy to award him a certificate of instruction, without which the way to important positions was closed.

Soon all these positions were filled, if not by superior minds at least by men sufficiently instructed to play a useful role in considering the most important questions. Most opinions rallied around the best principles, and what followed was a consistent system of Political Economy by which the authorities in the State regulated their operations, so that even with a change of men the maxims on important points remained the same; and since a constantly acting cause always produces its effect it came about that an honest comfort became very common, and excesses of wealth and poverty very rare, without injustices, social shocks, or disintegration.

Then most citizens, not so opulent as to wear out their lives in continual pleasures, but sufficiently at ease to be free from the discouragement and anguish of need, engaged in the moderate degree of work that leaves a person still in good spirits; they became accustomed to finding their fondest pleasures in the society of their family and a few friends; they no longer suffered from boredom and idleness and their train of accompanying vices. Living more soberly, they were of an equable humor, more disposed to the justice and good will that are the mother of all the other virtues.

To guard even more against the evils of idleness, they revived that law of Athens that required every citizen to declare his means of subsistence; and since some had the means of subsisting legitimately without working, the law was slightly modified to require each citizen to make known how he spent his time. This designation had to accompany his name and signature in all public acts, which were not valid without this formality. Hence, in the absence of a lucrative occupation, a name was often seen of a man engaged in researches in physics, or in experiments for the improvement of agriculture, or in giving a liberal education to a brother's orphan children. When there was a blatant discrepancy between a man's conduct and his professed activity, as the maker of a false declaration he was subjected to ridicule, and even more grave reproaches from which he would make great efforts to escape. If some affair or unforeseen circumstance revealed that a citizen had neglected to comply with this formality, his name was never again recalled without the qualification *useless man*.

By this means the Olbians brought it about that the love of gain should not be the only incentive to work. They knew that the love of gain is almost as much a danger as idleness. When too intense it excludes all others; it stifles the noble and disinterested feelings that should be part of a perfected human being. Thus among some peoples, and even among the inhabitants of some cities too much addicted to commerce, any idea except getting rich is regarded as foolish, and any sacrifice of money, time, or abilities is seen as a trap. Such a people may hire talented persons because it needs them, but it does not produce them itself. And since money cannot buy loyal friends and capable citizens, but only servitors with no feeling of attachment, it happens that nations of this kind, often quite soon, are subjected, dominated, and finally overthrown by those who follow different principles. What ever became of the Phoenicians and their successors the Carthaginians? We hardly know anything about their previous affairs except that they existed and devoted themselves exclusively to trade.

He then offers more modern examples: the Venetian and Dutch republics which had recently been occupied by the French republican armies, and even the United States, which in another connection he had suggested as a model to Europe.

Our own Europe offers several similar examples.

Venice, whose immense trade gave it the means to pay for numerous fleets and great armies, always commanded by a foreign general who was hardly more than a chief employee of its merchants—Venice carried on wars simultaneously against the Turks, the Empire, the Papacy, and France, but in the end a single battalion sufficed to take it.

Holland, the world's richest country and the most populous in proportion to size, was constantly the victim of all the more military powers of Europe that subjected it in turn and in the end disposed of its independence as they wished. And you in the United States of America, watch out for the general trend of thinking in your fine republic. If what they say of you is true you will become rich but you will not remain virtuous, and you will not long be free and independent.

The love of work must not be aroused only by the desire for gain. The happiness and even the preservation of society require that a certain number of persons cultivate the sciences, letters, and the fine arts, noble forms of knowledge that give birth to elevated feelings and the talents useful to society. Some writer in the depth of his modest study may work more effectively for the glory, power, and happiness of his country than some general who wins its battles. . . .

For the working class Say recommends thrift, to be facilitated by savings funds, *caisses de prévoyance*. He would himself be a leader in establishing savings banks in France some twenty years later.

For the working class the Olbians encouraged the love of work by other means, more useful to that class than to all other classes; they established *savings funds*. All who could put aside a small sum were enabled to place it in reserve in one of these funds every ten days; and hence, by the ordinary effect of the accumulation of interest, they saw it grow to the point where at their age of retirement they possessed a certain capital or life annuity. Almost all artisans entrusted some part of their wages to these funds, and instead of spending two or three days' wages out of ten on pleasure or intemperance they gave only one day to recreation. Pleasures enjoyed in the family are the least expensive, so that the Olbians preferred them as a way of saving, and when the day of rest came, they were not seen, as formerly in Olbia, in cabarets full of brutish drunkards swearing and cursing, but in the open country surrounding the city where father, mother, and children, happy and quietly joyful, walked to some rural meeting place to join friends like themselves. . . .

Several pages follow on the prohibition of lotteries and gambling houses and the wholesome recreations to replace them, and on the value of the unpretentious life.

The leading persons in Olbia expressed a great contempt for luxurious display, in order to reduce its effect on others. Simplicity of tastes and manners became the basis for preferment and consideration. The heads of State adopted a system of simplicity in their garments, their pleasures, and their social relations. Neither their domestic servants nor the soldiers of their guard showed a stupid regard for luxurious liveries. The body of the people gradually contracted the same habits, and there were no longer troops of imbeciles gawking at a diamond brooch or some such bauble. People were no longer esteemed in proportion to their consumption. And what happened? They consumed no more than was really necessary for their use or enjoyment. Luxury, attacked in its basis, which is opinion, gave place to a more widely spread comfort; and, as always happens, happiness increased as moral behavior was reformed.

In proportion as the taste for ostentation diminished, money moved in more laudable and productive directions. It went to give life to manufactures, and to make use of the industry and talent of those who were perishing from poverty without benefit to society or glory to the nation. The rich, less able to make a vain display of their great wealth, were afraid of not being respected. Some wanted their names attached to a public building, or to add to the general abundance by digging canals at their own expense. Some occupied themselves with opening a new great road, others with building a new seaport. In a word, they sought the glory of being called benefactors of the country, and their wealth was excused.

The Olbians would have been poor moralists if they had not understood the great influence of women on moral behavior. We owe to women our earliest knowledge and our final consolation. We are still indebted to them in our mature years. Their destiny is to rule us by the empire of benefits and pleasures, and where they are not virtuous it is impossible for us to become so. It is by the education of women that the education of men must begin.

Ten pages follow on women. A condescending male viewpoint is all too apparent. The "we" now means "we men." Women (or "they") are to be gentle, chaste, discreet, unassertive, and helpful. They should not thrust themselves into work suitable for men, nor venture into masculine sports and amusements. That women need not work at arduous jobs outside the home is noted as an achievement of an improved society. Yet there should be occupations reserved for women only, especially for those in need; these include women's hairdressing, the production of women's clothing and accompanying adornments, professional cooking, and the engraving of music.

Say grants that the public authorities should not pry into private life, and certainly not spy upon it. But he holds that some sort of social control over individual behavior is desirable. Thus the Olbians support the theater as an edifying institution. They see pageants and attend solemn public ceremonies. And as the ancient Romans had their "censors" the Olbians have an official board of moral inspectors, the *gardiens des moeurs*, who never inquire into any individual's motives but only examine his actions and their consequences, and award honors to those that are socially useful, and marks of dishonor to those that are socially pernicious.

Say closes his book with a description of further incentives to good behavior as they exist in Olbia. They are of three kinds: the very delights of the country itself, the building of monuments, and the placing on these monuments and almost everywhere else of inscriptions and placards on which the passerby could read, or be reminded of, the principles by which all should be guided. Olbia was a highly didactic and verbal society.

> . . . Until now I have considered happiness as a reward; it should also be regarded as a means. It softens the moral behavior that misfortune embitters. But joy is not happiness, and fireworks do no good whatever for moral science. True happiness consists not in pleasures but in a continuing feeling of satisfaction at all times. Hence the Olbians were convinced that they worked for moral behavior in multiplying the amenities and pleasantness of life.
>
> Their towns and villages were smiling, their habitations commodious, clean, and elegantly simple.

Here the author inserts another of his footnotes on the importance of economics:

> For this it is again comfort, and always comfort, that is needed; so that in the end it is useless to work on moral science before working on political economy. Otherwise you will have fluent speeches, or set up fine spectacles, after which the people will remain as vicious as they were because they are no less poor.

And following on the elegantly simple habitations:

> They also had many fountains and public gardens. Communication among the various provinces was easy. The people became more sociable and knowledge more widely diffused. The roads seemed like public walks. A wide path at a high elevation, with benches and shelters at intervals, made the strollers well-disposed and content. The simple citizen thought of his country as a mother, because she gave so many good things, and he took a few moments to reflect on the general good because the State had been concerned for his own good as a private person.
>
> But if the members of society could everywhere see the attention that society gave to them, they could also everywhere read the duties they owed to it.
>
> The language of monuments is understandable to all, for it addresses the heart and imagination. But the monuments of the Olbians seldom represented purely political duties, because political duties are abstract, based more on reasoning than on feeling. . . . The Olbians had only one Pantheon for great men [such as the Pantheon in Paris, recently converted from the church of Sainte-Geneviève] and several Pantheons for the virtues. But they did not simply raise a temple to friendship, and place over its door the words *To Friendship* inscribed in wood. Those entering it could feel again the soft and delightful sentiment of friendship and the duties it imposes. They saw the statues of [the famous friends] Orestes and Pylades, Henri and Sully, Montaigne and Laboétie. On their pedestals were engraved their main accomplishments and most memorable words. The walls of the temple were adorned with inscriptions, among them these:

Eight succinct statements are listed and here omitted, all dealing with friendship. But all this was not enough:

> A hundred other temples rose to celebrate other virtues. Nor was it enough for the interior of cities and temples to speak to the people. Similar sayings were found in other frequented places, among the walkways, and along the roads. Stone and bronze everywhere recounted praiseworthy actions or useful precepts. Statues and tombs taught what should be imitated, induce regret, or deserve homage. It was like what is reported by Plato, that one could take a course in moral science by walking through Attica.
>
> The most useful and most common precepts were chosen. We have seen how correct ideas in political economy are favorable to moral science. Hence ideas of this kind were mixed in with others. The agriculturalist, the merchant, the manufacturer, as he walked about, would en-

lighten himself on his true interests; he would find, for example, the following maxims which by their simple and lively language are easy to remember and repeat.

Eight maxims follow pertaining to political economy. Say attributes the first to La Fontaine, the second to Francis Bacon, and the final six to Benjamin Franklin, of which five had appeared in what he had written on Franklin in the *Décade philosophique* in 1794.

Heaven helps those who help themselves.
Follies of the morning are dearly bought in the evening.
If you love life waste no time, for time is what life is made of.
Laziness moves so slowly that poverty soon catches up.
Do you have something to do tomorrow? Do it today.
It costs more to support one vice than to raise two children.
Don't spend your money on something to regret.
If you will not listen to reason it will still make itself felt.

Other maxims applying to various occupations and social employments were located in appropriate places, but I think that those I have indicated are enough.

Heads of families gradually followed the examples provided by the public authorities. And examples that are at first imitated with difficulty are more infallibly imitated as time passes. In their own homes families could read sayings on the ordering of domestic life, and the children brought up on such maxims, and finding them confirmed by experience, made them their rule of conduct and transmitted them to their children. People were happy because they were well behaved. Men and nations cannot be so otherwise.

It is on this note of ubiquitous and intrusive moralizing that *Olbia* abruptly ends. Or rather, it does not end, for fifty pages of endnotes follow, each keyed to a phrase in the main text, of which it would be superfluous and tiresome even to give examples.

It is hard to know how much Say wrote *Olbia* in a playful mood, such as he had often exhibited in the *Décade philosophique*, and how much he meant to convey serious proposals for a better organization of society. He had a gift for doing both at the same time. In any case there are repeated references in *Olbia* to the need for correct ideas in political economy, and an insistence on the importance of productive work and on the value of the useful over the trivial, the ostentatious, or the otherworldly.

Chapter Three

THE FRUSTRATED ECONOMIST

THE YEARS from 1800 to 1814, during which Napoleon Bonaparte was First Consul and then Emperor, were also the years when Jean-Baptiste Say became an economist, though a frustrated one. He also became profoundly disillusioned with the course of events in France. This chapter will deal with the source of his frustrations, the next with his more distinctive contributions to economic thought.

On January 1, 1800 (or officially, 11 Nivôse of the Year VIII), two chambers called the Tribunate and the Legislative Body were installed as a lawmaking apparatus for the Consulate. Say became a member of the Tribunate at this time. Like many other republicans he at first had high hopes for the future. He served over two years at the Tribunate, but was then one of about twenty designated for elimination in a purge of August 1802. While in the Tribunate he worked on his *Treatise on Political Economy*, which he published in two volumes early in 1803. It sold well, but Bonaparte disapproved, and it could not be reprinted, although translations soon appeared in Germany and Spain. Bonaparte "suggested" revisions for a new French edition, and offered Say employment after his removal from the Tribunate, but Say declined his advances, and went instead into business for himself, setting up and managing a cotton-spinning factory in northern France. He remained at this occupation for eight years, removed from politics, and with his hopes both for post-Revolutionary France and for himself as an economist aborted. He even contemplated emigration to the United States.

The new regime of 1800 seemed promising at first. It realized some ideas that Say had expressed in 1795 in the *Décade philosophique* when he had commented on what became the constitution of the Year III. As Say would wish, the new constitution of the Year VIII made no invocation of the Supreme Being and began with no opening declaration of rights, though various civil rights were mentioned throughout its text. It was also relatively short. Mainly it only set up the three powers of government: executive, legislative, and judicial. The new upper house engaged in no debates, but only heard arguments from the lower house and the executive branch, and then either enacted or rejected what was proposed, as Say had advised in 1795. Strong powers were assigned to the First Consul in the person of Napoleon Bonaparte, somewhat as Say had observed in 1795 that in time of emergency there might be a kind of Committee of Public Safety for a limited period. That such an emergency existed in 1799 seemed clear to many republicans, with the constitution of 1795 collapsing and the war of the Second Coalition still in progress. Probably they believed that the special powers given to Bonaparte would be temporary.

Say's initially favorable attitude to the First Consul was evident in the preface to his *Olbie* published in 1800. It was shown again in December of that year in a speech delivered to the Legislative Body, or upper house, where he appeared as spokesman to support a proposal adopted by the Tribunate. The proposal was noncontroversial, the spokesman for the government said the same, and the Legislative Body duly enacted it into law. It decreed honors for the *Armée d'Orient*, the Army of the East that had been in Egypt for almost three years, cut off from France by Nelson's naval victory at Aboukir.

Say spoke with fervor because his brother, an engineering officer, had been killed in the Egyptian campaign, and also because he saw a civilizing mission for the French Republic in Egypt. Bonaparte had taken with him a great many civilians to serve as civil administrators, make scientific studies, and provide technical advice and assistance to the Egyptians. Say wanted these civilians to be as honorably recognized as the military. Bonaparte had proclaimed the liberation of Egypt from the Ottoman Empire, but Say even saw it as a future French colony, taking a more favorable view of colonies than he would express in his later writings.

He began, addressing the Legislative Body:

> The words spoken in this chamber will resound on the banks of the Nile. Our compatriots, separated for almost three years from their friends, their relatives, and their homeland . . . will endure the privations imposed on them more joyfully when they hear . . . that the legislators of France, the organs of the national will, applaud their civil and military virtues.
>
> It would be superfluous to retrace for you the great actions of the Army of the East from the assault on Alexandria to the battle of Heliopolis. . . .
>
> It would be wrong to try to diminish the glory of our soldiers by representing the Mamelukes, or the Muslims in general, as an easily dispersed horde of fighters. . . . Their numerous cavalry was mounted on Arabian horses, the best in the world. . . .

And with a glance at British malice and malignant disease:

> Also, the Ottomans were aided by the officers, troops, and ships of a European power always active to do us harm. They were aided by a deadly contagion that often mowed down heroes that the fury of combat had spared. . . .

I have mentioned our men of learning and the arts. How worthy they are to share in your eulogies! If our soldiers have offered the world for the first time the spectacle of an army bearing civilization rather than barbarism, organization rather than disorder, and trust rather than fright, our men of learning have been called upon to share in military dangers, to conquer knowledge at the point of the sword, and to show, also for the first time, how devotion to their country can be joined with love of the sciences, and military valor with cultivation of the arts.

Thanks to their labors, the ancient cradle of human knowledge will shine with a new brilliance. . . .

Who would dare calculate the future destinies of Egypt, destinies which even in this early stage terrify those masters of Bengal, those sovereign [British] merchants, who treat laborious nations as a lowly herd, and take their revenge on peaceful Hindus for obstacles set by European energy against their ambition and their greed?

If in this and preceding wars we have lost a part of our colonies [in North America and the West Indies] the courage of our Army of the East and ability of its chiefs have brought us another colony worth all the others. It is a mistake to think that Egypt lost its importance with the discovery of America and the passage around the Cape of Good Hope. It lost it to domination by barbarians. More accessible than other colonies of European peoples, Egypt produces everything that can be brought from the Antilles. In the hands of a civilized nation it provides a shorter and more secure means of communicating with the peoples of the Orient; and it can be reasonably hoped, given the point to which the mechanical arts and theory of canals are now perfected, that an early connection between the Nile and the Red Sea can be opened. Alexandria will be as in former times the entrepôt for an immense trade. If the ships of Christopher Columbus discovered new lands in the West, let us not forget that those of Vasco da Gama at about the same time pushed back the limits of the known world in the opposite direction, and that by the effect of these twofold discoveries Egypt is still the center of the world.

It will remain in our hands; I swear it by the genius of Bonaparte and of the Republic. And you, our soldiers, generals, artists, men of learning, and administrators attached to the Army of the East, you are fulfilling your destinies. Your brothers in arms in Europe are enforcing peace upon the powers in league against your security, and peace will put an end to your sacrifices while nothing can put an end to your glory.

The Army of the East had a short time to enjoy its honors. A few weeks after Say's speech it went out of existence as an organized body, defeated by a British expeditionary force to which it was obliged to surrender. Egypt became no colony of the French. But the three-year

French occupation had widespread and lasting effects, precipitating attempts at modernization by the Ottomans, and by its detailed reports and exact drawings, which were soon published, virtually creating the science of Egyptology.

Say seldom spoke in the Tribunate, but he was an active member of its finance committee. In April 1802 the committee asked Say to prepare a report to be made to the full Tribunate. The government had requested permission to spend an additional 300 million francs in anticipation of taxes to be collected in the following year XI (beginning in September 1802), but without specifying the purposes for which this money would be spent. Say composed a report in which, after commenting on French public finance for the past century, he argued for stricter budgetary controls.

The first of the frustrations that could be attributed to Bonaparte soon followed. The committee decided not to use Say's draft, fearing that the Tribunate's acceptance of it would be displeasing to the First Consul. Many in the Tribunate in 1802 approved of what Bonaparte was then doing, but some did not, and although it still enjoyed some freedom of speech its position was precarious. (It was purged a few months later and suppressed in 1807.) It therefore adopted a bland resolution for action by the Legislative Body, and the government received its 300 million francs on its own terms.

Say's draft, remaining unpublished, was found among his papers by his son and son-in-law and included in their collection of his writings in 1848. His opinions were nevertheless known in 1802, and were among the reasons for his elimination from the Tribunate. They reflect his thinking while working on his treatise on economics. His main point was that in a real budget the expenses should not be lumped together but particularized in some detail.

> ... In nations where taxes are regarded as willingly made contributions it is customary for governments first to justify the need for expenditures and then to explain the use made of the funds. It is known that in England the first of these requirements is fulfilled by what is called the *Budget*, a barbarous word even in English, where it has been turned from its original meaning, and which we could advantageously replace by calling the thing by its name: the balance of the needs and resources of the State.
>
> The United States of America follow a similar procedure, having adopted the English system of legislation without its abuses. This is the more noteworthy since the United States are the only nation I know of where the government is in no need of asking the legislature for money, since the customs revenue last year was sufficient to pay interest on the public debt and all expenses of the Union.

In France, the Constituent Assembly for the first time provided a basis for sound finance in our legislation; I say "basis" only, for it was unable to do more. We owe it thanks at least for having rejected the fiscal spirit that dominated in France before it, whose deplorable ingenuity was not in reducing expenditure to the level of strict necessity but in raising the burden of taxation as much as it could. . . .

The monarchical constitution of 1791 delegated the power of determining public expenditures exclusively to the legislative body, and ordered the several ministries to present to it, at the opening of each session, a view of the needs of their departments.

We should look for no models or enlightenment in the years that followed. Needs multiplied beyond measure. Resources were in a state of disaster, and arose from sublime sacrifices and appalling misfortunes. It was only with the constitution of the Year III [1795] that an appearance of order followed the greatest financial disorder known to history. . . .

But chaos again ensued, and we find Say in May 1802 making about the last laudatory reference to Napoleon that he ever wrote, whether from conviction, tact, or expediency cannot be known.

To restore hope and repress abuses it took no less than the powerful hand of the great man who has forced peace upon our last and most obstinate enemies. Our new constitution lays a foundation for a better financial order. Its article 45 directs that an annual law should determine the amount of receipts and expenses of the State. Its article 56 stipulates that the minister of the public treasury *may order no payment except by virtue of a law and in the amount determined by law for a category of expenses.* This necessity implies that each category of expense has been specified and authorized in advance.

But the determination of ordinary expenses was made almost impossible by the high expectations that the new government had in mind, by the need of concealing from a sharp-eyed enemy the steps that his obstinacy forced us to take, and by the uncertainty of events at a time when a part of Europe refused to render the unanimous homage that it now makes to the power of the nation and the wisdom of its chief magistrate.

For two years, therefore (to paraphrase Say), the legislative power has allowed the executive to overspend the amount originally authorized. Now the government again requests authorization to preempt 300 million francs on the taxes to be raised next year. But with peace now made even with England (it lasted only a year) and so all Europe now at peace, and with the new organs of government functioning more smoothly, we should consider putting our public finance on a more secure foundation.

Then the nation will enjoy the advantage of moderating its expenditures without being parsimonious. For you will observe, members of the Tribunate, that parsimony is most often the consequence not of economy but of profusion. It is when we wish to give too much to one kind of need that another gets too little, or when for each kind of expenditure we do not set in advance the bounds at which it should stop. When, on the contrary, we keep these bounds in mind as we proceed through the year it is unusual to reach the line we have already drawn. The best time to anticipate, balance, and regularize the use of funds is at the moment when they are authorized. Once an undertaking has begun it must be finished at whatever cost. It cannot be opposed without compromising the glory and security of the State; the deliberative bodies must give their approval unless they wish to take a disaffected attitude that is painful and even odious for men concerned with the public good and the need of tranquility.

Allow me also to observe, members of the Tribunate, that fixing the sum of expenditures and appropriation of revenues will bring about a restoration of public credit, to which the operations of government during the present session are already strongly contributing. The firm resolution it is showing and the measures of order that it takes to assure payment of the debt will produce a much greater confidence in its other commitments, and this confidence will be complete when all those who provide their goods or their time for public purposes can see in advance the payment listed among liabilities of the State, and see also in a parallel column the funds designated for this purpose. There will be no more of those burdensome arrangements in which the provider adds for insurance against risk to the price of what he provides, and no more of those difficulties and delays which often discourage the honest businessman from dealing with agents of the nation. The government, in its purchases, will have an advantage over the best private firms, because it is the largest of all consumers.

These opinions of Say's, though not publicly recorded at the time, led to his inclusion in the purge of the Tribunate in August 1802.

We come now to the principal work, the *chef d'oeuvre*, the *Treatise* of 1803, never translated into English and virtually suppressed by Bonaparte at the time. Its full title was *A Treatise on Political Economy, or Simple exposition of the way in which wealth is formed, distributed and consumed*. It was one of the main channels through which the thought of Adam Smith was eventually made known to Europe, and by its title gave more explicit attention to distribution and consumption than Smith had done.

The appearance of the *Treatise* in two volumes of over a thousand pages makes meaningful selection in a brief space somewhat arbitrary. We confine ourselves to a few items chosen for two kinds of reasons. In the present chapter we include a few passages that were contrary to Bonaparte's way of thinking, and in the next a few more purely economic concepts for whose introduction into economic thought Say was influential.

There was much that Say and Bonaparte might agree on—that personal security and internal peace were prerequisite to any good society; that all armed force should be in the hands of the state; that laws should be short, clear, and simple (Bonaparte's codes); that a country should have sound money, without the inflation that had occurred during the Revolution; that the legal privileges of the Old Regime had been bad; that government should support education and even pay for its highest branches; that it should build and maintain roads, bridges, harbors, city streets, and facilities for urban sewage and water supply; but that economic production and distribution should be carried on by private citizens as property owners in a market economy, with a freedom of exchange within national borders. Both, in their separate ways, were upholders of a "bourgeois" or civil society.

But they clearly differed, in some ways obviously, in others only in nuances. Bonaparte made wars; Say deplored them. The First Consul and Emperor had a faith in leadership by technocrats and trained civil servants which Say did not share. He imposed more press controls than Say would desire. He favored protective tariffs; Say preferred international freedom of trade. He raised taxes without compunction; Say saw them as necessary within limits but always as burdens on producers and consumers. These differences were too pervasive to exhibit by selected quotations.

One difference, or at least matter that Bonaparte may have found doubtful or distasteful, was Say's belief that political economy was a science. It can only be remarked in Bonaparte's favor that many people from that day to this have had the same opinion of economics, from practitioners of the natural and exact sciences through the literary and artistic worlds to ordinary persons of various political persuasions. Bonaparte enforced his own views by dissolving the Class of Moral and Political Sciences in the National Institute, which included political economy, in January 1803, shortly before the appearance of Say's *Treatise.* Say began his book on the first page of the Introduction with words that Bonaparte would call those of an Ideologue. If political economy was a science it might inhibit a government's freedom of action.

It may be useful for the progress of a science to determine clearly the field over which its inquiries should extend and the objects it proposes to study. Otherwise we seize haphazardly on a number of truths without knowing the connections between them, and many errors in which we cannot discover the fallacy.

Until Adam Smith wrote there was confusion between Politics, properly understood as the science of government, and Political Economy which shows how wealth is formed, distributed, and consumed. . . .

It seems that writers since Smith have consistently distinguished between two bodies of doctrine, reserving the term Political Economy for the science that treats the wealth of nations, and the term Politics, taken by itself, to designate the relation between a government and its people and among governments themselves.

But Smith and his followers have not been equally cautious with another kind of confusion that must be cleared up.

In Political Economy, as in physics, and indeed in everything else, thinkers have constructed systems before establishing truths, for a system is more easily built than a truth is discovered. But our science has benefited from the excellent methods that have brought progress in the other sciences. It now admits only the *rigorous consequences of facts carefully observed*, and rejects the prejudices and authorities which, in science as in moral philosophy, formerly interposed between the observer and the truth.

It has not been adequately noted that there are two kinds of facts. There are *general* or *constant* facts, and *particular* or *variable* facts. General facts are the result of the action of laws of nature in similar cases. Particular facts are also results of action of the laws of nature, which are never violated, but they are the result of several actions modified by each other in a particular case. All are incontestable even when they seem to be in contradiction. In physics it is a general fact that heavy bodies fall to the earth. Yet the water in our fountains spurts upward and remains there. The particular fact of the fountain is an effect in which the laws of equilibrium combine with those of gravity without subverting them. . . .

Political Economy has solid foundations when its basic principles are rigorous deductions from incontestable general facts. Such general facts are indeed based on the observation of particular facts, when results are found to be constant each time a particular fact is observed. A new particular fact cannot abrogate a general fact, because we can never be sure that some unknown circumstance may not have made a difference. I see a feather lightly floating in the air and sometimes tossing up and down before falling to the ground. Should I conclude that gravitation does not exist for it? I would be mistaken. In Political Economy it is a general fact that the interest on money is proportionate to the risk incurred by the lender. Should I conclude that the principle is false because I have seen loans made at a low rate of interest in some very risky cases? The lender may have not known the risk, or some sense of obligation may have made him willing to accept a sacrifice. A thousand circumstances may disturb the action of the principal law, which though real we are unable to recognize, and which will assert itself as soon as the causes of perturbation, which are the effect of some other general law, cease to operate. In any case, how few particular facts are well attested! How few are observed together with all their circumstances! And even supposing them well attested, observed, and described, how many of them prove nothing, or prove the opposite of what is claimed?

Thus it happens that the most extravagant opinions have been supported by facts, and that by facts the public authorities have often been misled. . . .

Political Economy, like the exact sciences, is composed of a small number of fundamental principles and a great many corollaries that follow from these principles. . . .

These principles are not the work of men; they derive from the nature of things. They are not established; they are found. They govern lawmakers and princes, who never violate them with impunity. . . .

Bonaparte, who has been called the last of the eighteenth-century enlightened despots, must also have disliked Say's claim that the new science should be made understandable to all segments of the population. If not exactly a popularizer, Say clearly meant his *Treatise* to reach a very wide audience, and by implication provide a basis for criticism of official policies.

It has almost always been thought that Political Economy should be useful, at most, in clarifying some questions for a small number of men occupied with the affairs of state. It has not been sufficiently noticed that, since almost everyone takes part in the formation of wealth and everyone without exception takes part in its consumption, there is no one whose behavior does not affect, in varying degrees, both his own wealth and the general wealth, and hence the fate both of himself and of the state. We have not sufficiently seen in Political Economy what it really is, even for peoples under an arbitrary rule—it is everybody's business.

I know that the enlightenment of persons in high position is of greater consequence than that of simple private persons, because their decisions affect many people's lives; but can the powerful themselves be truly enlightened when ordinary private persons are not? This question is well worth asking.

It is in the middling class, far from the cares and pleasures of greatness, far from the sufferings of the poor; it is in this class that we find respectable fortunes, leisure mixed with the habit of work, free exchange of friendship, and a taste for reading and travel; it is in this class, I say, that enlightenment begins and from which it spreads to both great persons and the common people, for the great and the plain people have no time for thoughtful reflection; they accept a truth only when it comes to them as an axiom with no farther need of proofs. Even if a monarch and his principal ministers should be familiar with the principles on which the prosperity of nations is based, of what use would their knowledge be to them if they were not supported at all levels of government by men able to understand them, share their views, and realize their objectives? The prosperity of a town or province may sometimes depend on the work of a bureau, and a very subordinate official by bringing about an important decision often has a greater influence than the lawmaker himself.

And finally, even supposing that those taking part in the management of public affairs might be competent in Political Economy (which is altogether improbable), what resistance would they not encounter in fulfilling their best goals? What obstacles in the prejudices of the very persons who would benefit from their operations?

For a nation to enjoy the advantages of a good economic system it is not enough for its leaders to know how to adopt the best plans. It is still necessary for the nation to be in a condition to receive them. . . .

Useful knowledge should be within the ability of everyone to understand, even those with little education if only they are willing to give me their attention. An author must lead from simple truths to the most abstract principles of Political Economy. My efforts in this direction will be appreciated by those already instructed in the subject. I beg them to excuse the repetition of things they know very well. . . .

He issues a warning against an excessive use of mathematics in Political Economy, because Political Economy is concerned with the action of human beings.

It will seem more difficult to make these ideas generally understood if we consider that Political Economy like mathematics is founded on an abstraction; the one on *magnitude*, the other on *value*. Since values can be *more* or *less*, they are within the domain of mathematics, but since they are subject to human will, abilities, and needs they are within the domain of moral science. And this, let it be said in passing, is why it is superfluous to apply algebraic formulas to demonstrations in Political Economy. None of its quantities is susceptible to exact estimation. . . .

The dryness and obscurity of books on Political Economy have made them much less easy to study. But is this the fault of the science, or of those who profess it? Its basic observations are understandable to everybody, and the consequences that it deduces are within the reach of all who will take the trouble to follow a line of reasoning. It can be made as clear as the other sciences, and a science should not be thought arid which speaks to men of their production, i.e., the miracles of their industry, and of their consumption, i.e., their enjoyments.

Education was another matter on which Say and Bonaparte disagreed. It followed from Say's way of thinking, in which everybody should have some understanding of economics, that all social classes should have some degree of schooling. Bonaparte, in his reorganization of the schools, was mainly concerned with the formation of a leadership and professional class in his lycées and other secondary schools and the higher faculties of his university. In none of these did he provide for any teaching of economics. He left elementary education to be financed voluntarily by the church, private philanthropy, or local governments if they so wished. Say, like Adam Smith, thought it should be paid for by the state. He included it in a chapter on "establishments" to be maintained at public expense, such as the armed forces, the civil service, and some kinds of poor relief. Observing, like Adam Smith, that with the division of labor the common workman was reduced to a dull, repetitious, and low-paying job, he saw all the more need for common schooling. It was necessary for "civilization," another new word at the time.

But the role of the unskilled worker in the productive mechanisms of society reduces his earnings almost to a subsistence level. At the most he can barely bring up his children; he will not give them as much instruction as we suppose necessary for the good of the social order. If society wishes to have the advantage of such instruction for this class it must pay for it at its own expense.

This is accomplished in elementary schools where one learns to read, write, and calculate. Such knowledge is the basis of all others, and is enough to civilize the most simple worker. Indeed, a nation is not civilized, and hence cannot enjoy the advantages of civilization, unless everyone knows how to read, write, and calculate. Otherwise a nation has not yet risen from barbarism. I will add that with such knowledge no exceptional aptitude or extraordinary talent, whose development may be highly profitable to society, can remain buried and neglected. The ability to read puts the most humble citizen, at little expense, in contact with what the world has most significantly produced in the line of activity to which he feels called by his own genius. Nor should women be without this elementary instruction, for it is no less important for them to be civilized, since they are only too often the only teachers of their children.

Say's economics is no apology for the status quo. He thinks the world full of ignorance and injustice, but that a new age may be dawning with the new nineteenth century. No attention should be paid to the thoughtless rich or to anyone who imagines the existing form of society to be the only one possible.

Although several nations of Europe are flourishing in appearance, and although some, like England, spend fourteen hundred million a year on their public expenses alone, we should not suppose that their situation leaves nothing to be desired. A rich Sybarite, living at will in his town house or country home, enjoying the utmost indulgences at great expense in either place, moving conveniently and speedily wherever his caprice may take him, having at his disposal the arms and talents of a great many servants and admirers, and wearing out ten horses for his own amusement, may indeed think that things go very well and that Political Economy has reached perfection. But if you consider that in the *most prosperous* countries not one individual in a hundred thousand can accumulate such enjoyments, and that the emaciation of poverty goes along with the fatness of opulence, the inescapable labor of some with the idleness of others, hovels with colonnades, rags with the emblems of luxury, in a word useless profusion with the most urgent needs, you will hardly think superfluous the studies made to find the causes of these evils and the remedies to which they are susceptible.

Some people who have done very well in this social order will find arguments to justify it in the light of reason. Perhaps if they were to draw a new lot in a lottery held tomorrow, assigning them a different place in society, they would find much to be improved.

Others, unable to conceive of a better social state, assert that it cannot exist. They concede that there are evils in the social order, but console themselves by saying that things cannot be otherwise. They remind one of that emperor of Japan who thought he would die of laughter on hearing that the Dutch had no king. The Iroquois and Algonquins cannot imagine going to war without roasting their prisoners. . . .

We are entering on a century destined for a glory that it will share with no others. How many so-called civilized nations are still ignorant and barbarous! Travel through whole provinces, question a hundred persons, a thousand, ten thousand, and you will hardly find one or two who have an inkling of the higher forms of knowledge on which our age prides itself. Perhaps it is for the nineteenth century to perfect the application of such knowledge. We may see that more gifted minds, after expanding the bounds of theory, will find ways to bring important truths to those of more modest understanding. Then ordinary people, in their daily lives and in the most common productive activities, will be guided by sound ideas; the merchant, the government official, even the artisan will not know everything but they will know what they ought to know; and we shall less often see the sad spectacle of absurdities and false steps so fatal to the happiness of individuals and the prosperity of nations.

It is with these words that Say's Introduction to his *Treatise* of 1803 concludes. It is easy to see what in this Introduction Bonaparte might not want to hear, especially concerning the rich Sybarite and the impoverished multitude, whose sufferings were to be relieved by "science," and by a science made known to "everybody," though most especially to the middle classes. Much of what Say said was to be expressed later by socialists in their critique of classical economics and of capitalism. Say offered political economy (no one said "economics" or "capitalism" until about 1850) as a cure for poverty. He restated and amplified his Introduction with minor alterations in later editions of his book. It may be significant that the English translator of 1821 omitted Say's introduction, replacing it with one of his own, and that Say in writing to this translator, while thanking him, regretted the absence of what he considered to be important. The American editor of the English translation, Clement Biddle, in fact included Say's introduction, which he translated himself.

Other thoughts not to be relished by the First Consul and Emperor may be found in the thousand pages of the *Treatise* after the introduction. For example, he has a good word to say on the French Revolution (which indeed Bonaparte might share), but with the thought, as with later socialists, that the Revolution had not gone far enough since it still left too many people in poverty. The following passage occurs in connection with a criticism of Adam Smith on the matter of "savings" in the economist's sense of the word.

Adam Smith thinks that the extravagance and incompetence of both private persons and custodians of the public purse are more than made up for by the frugality of most citizens and their concern for their own interests. It seems certain that in our time all the European nations are growing in opulence, which could not happen unless each nation, on the whole, consumed less than it produced. Even modern revolutions, not having been followed by general invasions and prolonged ravages, as older revolutions were, and having on the other hand destroyed old prejudices, sharpened our understanding, and abolished vexatious barriers, seem to have been more favorable than unfavorable to the progress of opulence. But as for this frugality for which Smith gives private persons the honor, is it not forced upon the most numerous class? Is it so certain that the share of this class in products is exactly proportioned to the part it plays in production? In what are considered the richest countries how many people live in perpetual want! There are many households, in town and country, where the whole of life consists of privations, and where a family is surrounded by all that can arouse desires but is reduced to satisfying its grossest needs, as if living in a time of barbarism among the most indigent nations.

I conclude that although there are undoubtedly savings each year in almost all the European states, these savings are not made by the curtailment of useless consumption, as good policy and humanity would wish, but by inadequate satisfaction of actual needs; and this is an indictment of the economic system of many governments.

As an example of the useless consumption that might best be curtailed, Say cited the lavish building and splendid court of Louis XIV and his successors at Versailles, of which Bonaparte could hardly be accused in 1803, but which he already admired, and was to imitate in the next ten years in his monumental building in Paris, his ostentatious imperial court, and the pompous titles and extravagant gifts that he bestowed on his principal followers. Say had already said in his utopia of 1800 that his Olbians, as they lost their "taste for ostentation," invested more in manufactures and other productive activities.

The distinction between useful and useless consumption is developed at length in the final fifth of the *Treatise* of 1803, where it occupies the whole of Book Five. We hear further echoes from *Olbia*: political economy is a moral science, existing society is unjust, extravagant wealth and dire poverty are both bad, and there is economic wisdom in the maxims of Poor Richard.

By real needs I understand those that concern our very existence, our health, and the contentment of the largest number of people. They are the opposite of needs for fastidious sensory pleasure, or that arise merely from opinion or caprice. Thus the consumption of a nation will be well-ordered if it possesses things that are convenient rather than splendid, much linen but little lace, wholesome and abundant food instead of choicely concocted dishes, and good clothing but no embroidery. In such a nation the public establishments will be useful but not ostentatious, the indigent will see no well-appointed hospices but will find assured assistance, the roads will not be twice as wide as necessary but the inns will be well kept, the towns will perhaps show no grand edifices but the citizens will walk safely on the sidewalks.

The luxury of display brings only a hollow satisfaction, but there is a real satisfaction in the luxury of convenience, if I may so call it. The latter is less expensive and so consumes less. The former knows no limits; it grows upon a person with no motive except that he sees it growing in others. It can thus expand progressively to infinity. In the words of Franklin's Poor Richard: "Pride is a beggar that cries as loudly as need, but is infinitely more insatiable." . . .

It is to be observed that too great an inequality of fortunes is contrary to all the kinds of consumption that we should regard as desirable. In proportion as private fortunes are unequal there is more satisfaction of artificial needs and less of real ones. Quick consumption multiplies; never, in ancient Rome, did men like Lucullus and Heliogabalus think they had devoured or spoiled enough. Where great wealth and great poverty are found together there is more immoral consumption. Society divides into a few who have great enjoyments and a greater number who envy them and do all they can to imitate them. Any means of getting into the upper class seems good, and there are as few scruples on the means of pleasure as on the amassing of wealth.

These words, carried on into later editions of the *Treatise*, provoked a critical footnote from the English translator, who believed that Say was here in error, since the prospect of great enrichment was a necessary incentive to actions that advanced the wealth of society as a whole. Say went on, continuing the above:

In every country the government exerts a very great influence on habits of consumption, not only because it must decide on the nature of public consumption, but because its example and its preferences guide consumption by private persons. . . .A prince who knows the prodigious influence of his example on the conduct of his fellow citizens, and the influence of their conduct on the national prosperity and manners, will form a very high idea of his duties.

Among unproductive forms of consumption, undoubtedly the most misunderstood are those that produce evils and vexations instead of expected pleasures. Such are the excesses of intemperance, and such in the class of public consumption are wars undertaken for revenge, as when Louis XIV declared war on a Dutch journalist, or wars for empty glory which usually end up in shame and hatred. In any case such wars are an affliction less by the losses they cause in the domain of Political Economy than by the loss of virtues and talents that they cut down forever. Such losses are a tribute that a country, and the families within it, will pay with pain in time of necessity, but they are appalling when they pay only for the ineptitude, frivolity, and passions of great men. . . .

Louis XIV, toward the end of his reign, after exhausting the resources of his fine kingdom, created [and sold] all manner of ridiculous offices. . . . But such expedients, as miserable in yielding revenue as they were ruinous in their effects, only retarded for a time the catastrophe into which prodigal governments are bound to fall. We remember the dissipation under the regency of Anne of Austria and those of the latter years of her son [Louis XIV], and since then the scandalous embarrassments of the Regency, and finally the Revolution, a terrible example, productive of great results but also of many misfortunes. *When you will not listen to reason*, said Franklin, *it will still make itself felt.*

Such exhortations, however prophetic, could hardly be pleasing to Napoleon Bonaparte, whose moral ideas, if they may be called such, turned more on honor, courage, and a quest for glory, and whose grandiose ambitions were unlikely to be deterred by the maxims of Benjamin Franklin.

On another matter, slavery in the colonies, Say's views were flatly contrary to Bonaparte's. In Saint-Domingue, the modern Haiti, a slave rebellion in 1791 had been so successful that the National Convention in 1794 decreed the abolition of slavery in all French possessions. In the ensuing conflicts among blacks, mulattoes, French, Spanish, and British, a former slave, Toussaint l'Ouverture, had proclaimed an independent black republic, been captured by the French, and died in a prison in France in 1803, at about the very time when Say's *Treatise* was published. Bonaparte then took steps to reintroduce slavery in the French West Indies.

Say's comments on slavery come in two places in the *Treatise*, once in a chapter on colonies, and again in a passage on the incomes of the various kinds of persons engaged in production. He begins the chapter on colonies by distinguishing two kinds, the ancient and the modern. In the ancient system, of which the Greeks were the prime example, whole families went out in sizeable groups from a mother city or country, the *metropole*, to establish themselves in a distant place with the expectation of remaining there for generations into the future. They soon prospered, since they took with them some capital, if only in their tools, industrious habits, and other elements of the civilization from which they came, to be put to work on thinly inhabited if not altogether free land. Say noted in 1803 only one exception to this "ancient" system in modern times; it was the European colonies in North America which became the United States. In later editions he made this exception in more general terms, as if to allow for places like Canada.

I come now to the colonies formed by the modern colonial system. Their founders were mostly adventurers not in search of an adoptive country but of a fortune to be taken back and enjoyed in the country from which they came. The first of them found what satisfied their greed, great as it was, on the one hand in the Antilles, Mexico, and

Peru, and later in Brazil, and on the other hand in the east Indies. Their successors found less gold and silver, but soon saw that the soil of several colonies could produce other precious goods less susceptible to exhaustion, such as sugar, indigo, cotton, coffee, etc. These late-comers shared somewhat in the spirit of their predecessors, but the progress of European civilization and the authority of the home governments regularized the impact of their efforts to a certain extent. Landed property became secure and large amounts of capital became necessary for its exploitation. But they still preserved in varying degree the spirit of return, the desire not to live on their lands and leave a happy family and spotless reputation at death, but a taste for large gains so as to go off and enjoy their immense profits elsewhere. This motive introduced violent methods of exploitation, of which the most important was slavery.

That slavery also existed in the United States, the "exception" to the modern system, is overlooked by Say at this point. It is true that the large plantation owners of the American South, unlike those in the French and British Caribbean islands, conformed to Say's "ancient" pattern in having no wish to return to a home country to enjoy their wealth. Say goes on with economic arguments against slavery:

> What is the effect of slavery with respect to production?
>
> I have no doubt that it greatly increases it, or at least that in the labor of the slave the excess of his product over his consumption is much greater than in the labor of a free man. . . .
>
> The maintenance of a slave is as cheap as his toil is great. It is of no concern to the master that he should enjoy life; it is enough if he survives. In the Antilles, a pair of trousers and a shirt or jacket constitute his wardrobe; his dwelling is a hut without furniture; his food is manioc, to which good masters sometimes add a bit of dried cod. . . .
>
> The upkeep of a Negro in the Antilles in the most humanely managed plantations comes to no more than 300 francs a year, to which we can add the interest on his price of purchase, and call this interest ten percent since it is on a lifetime asset only. The price of an ordinary Negro being about 2,000 francs, the interest would be 200 francs a year at the highest. Hence we can estimate that each Negro costs the owner about 500 francs a year. Now compare the annual consumption of a Negro with that of a free worker in the same colonies. The most unskilled, that is those whose ability is no greater than that of a Negro slave, are paid from five to seven francs a day and sometimes more. Taking six francs as the average, and allowing for only 300 working days in the year, we reach a sum of 1,800 francs for their annual wages. . . . We have seen that a slave can be kept for 500. . . .

Say next devotes several pages to refuting the belief of Adam Smith, Turgot, and others, who had maintained that slave labor was less profitable than free labor, which implied that it might eventually peaceably disappear. This argument persisted well into the nineteenth century in both Europe and the United States among antislavery publicists who detested slavery as much as Say did. Indeed, a British antislavery society in the 1820s took issue with Say on this point, since it still appeared in Say's fourth edition from which the translation into English was made. The society feared that if slavery was really profitable it would be harder to extinguish. Say stuck to his opinion on the profitability of slavery in later editions of the *Treatise*, but he also more vehemently condemned it on other grounds, declaring that it degraded both masters and slaves, that wherever it existed all faculties of mind were stunted, and that "those states of the North American Union that have proscribed slavery are making the largest strides toward national prosperity."

To recur to what he said in 1803, after debating with Adam Smith and Turgot:

> I think then I can affirm that slave labor is less costly than free labor, and even affirm that it is more productive if only it is managed by free men. That is the source of the huge profits of planters in the Antilles. They know what they are doing when they argue that their islands can only be cultivated by slaves; they mean that their lands can only by this means yield 15 or 18 percent of their price. It remains to be seen whether the advantage of procuring 18 percent on investment for a few private citizens is enough to authorize the most shameful traffic in which human beings have ever engaged, the trade in their fellow creatures. It is for such profits that a million men are deprived of the precious privilege of following their own inclinations and having a choice in the use of their natural faculties. . . .
>
> I know that if the profits of the planters were not so great there would be few who would wish to brave an inconvenient and unhealthful climate, and to expatriate themselves to procure for us sugar, coffee, and indigo. I know that the islands may become what they inevitably will one day be, colonies like those of the ancients, truly adoptive countries, where people will no longer go to make a fortune but to live there, bring up a family there, and die there.

The other place in the *Treatise* where Say dwells on slavery is in a series of chapters on categories of persons involved in productive activity. There are five such categories: the man with capital to invest, the man of knowledge, the man of enterprise, the ordinary worker, and the slave. The chapters explain the differences of "profits," by which he here means income, among the categories in terms of the rarity or abundance of what they offer, that is, supply, and of the need of others for such offerings, that is, demand. The slave is of course by far the poorest. The following is the short chapter in its entirety.

ON THE PROFITS OF THE SLAVE

It seems that there may be a contradiction between these two words, and that since all a slave's property belongs to his master his income must be part of the master's income. Hence I will count as profits of the slave only what the master can no further withhold from him, or in other words the total of his actual consumption. The slave's annual income is composed of all values consumed by him in a year.

This income is the most miserable of all, for it does not include even what is needed to maintain the slaves as a class. A free worker, however low his wage, must be able to support a family with this wage; otherwise the class of workers would decrease and the demand for their labor would soon restore the wage to the level needed to restore the class. But the class of slaves is maintained at the expense of the masters. It is the masters who pay both for the raising of Negro children and to lay out the capital for obtaining an adult.

Probably the price of a Negro newly brought to the Antilles is less than the capital needed to raise one on the spot. Otherwise the owners would multiply the slaves on their plantations rather than buy them in the trade. But doesn't this show how bad the conditions on most plantations are? Should the consumption of a Negro child until the age of ten cost only 2,000 francs, the usual price of a Negro in the trade? I count only the consumption until this age, after which it can be balanced by the services he can render. We know that at the adult age the slave's labor pays for very large profits in addition to his upkeep and the interest on his purchase price.

It is true that when slaves are raised on the plantations their mortality is a cost to the owner, but even if the rate of mortality is estimated at one-fourth it leaves three-fourths of the purchase price, or 1,500 francs, for raising a Negro to age ten. The proportion may be higher, but it makes me suspect that conditions on the plantation are not what they might be. I am confirmed in this idea by the experience of a convent of Dominican fathers in Martinique. These men of religion, who unlike other planters were not animated by an intention to return to the home country, took the most paternal care of their plantation; they found it best to raise their own Negroes for its cultivation; they purchased none, and enjoyed the advantage of having slaves accustomed to the climate and with less to complain of than those who had been torn away from their own country, their families, and their usual habits.

How long will books on Political Economy have to contain chapters such as this one?

This parting question was answered by Say himself. In the second and later editions of his *Treatise*, this chapter was omitted. One might suppose that he omitted it to avoid useless controversy with his readers, since slavery remained in existence in the Caribbean islands and the United States until after his death in 1832, although the transatlantic or directly African slave trade was then illegal but hardly nonexistent. In fact, however, the later editions continued to include the more extensive treatment of slavery in connection with colonies, as presented here in preceding pages, and in some passages with more outspoken disapproval than in the first edition. Readers of the English translation, in its long continuing American reprints, could plainly see Say's strong antislavery sentiments. Some of what he said, as in arguing that it cost more to raise slaves locally than to import them, applied much less to the United States than to the West Indies, since almost all blacks in the antebellum United States had been in America for generations; very few were recent "imports."

To summarize, there was much in Say's treatise that Bonaparte might not like. His book was published, but could not be reprinted. Bonaparte tried to win him over, offered him ideas for a new edition, and when these were rejected even named him for a post in the tax collection service, which Say refused. But the Napoleonic regime was far from totalitarian; a strong civil society existed beneath it; and Say easily moved over into private business, in which he prospered for several years.

His ideas as presented in this chapter were not his alone. He himself saw Adam Smith as the founder of a new science. There were others who opposed extravagant grandeur and colonial slavery, and some who believed, like the French revolutionaries, that elementary schools should be paid for by the state. We turn next to ideas in economics in which Say was more of an innovator.

Chapter Four

THE INNOVATIVE ECONOMIST

LESS LIKELY to offend Bonaparte, who might have thought them innocuously theoretical, were four concepts for whose introduction into economic thought Say has been credited by historians of the subject. Each can be identified by a word or two: "utility," "services" (which he called "immaterial products"), "entrepreneur," and "Say's Law," though of course Say himself never used any such expression. All occur in the first edition of the *Treatise*, and were developed in later editions and in Say's other writings. We illustrate them here by excerpts from the *Treatise* of 1803. These are followed by passages in which he applies his economic ideas to the then much discussed problems of population. The chapter concludes with an account of his years of reluctant silence, eventuating in thoughts of emigration to America as expressed in an exchange of letters with Thomas Jefferson.

On "utility" there is no sign that Say in 1803 had read or been influenced by the writings of Jeremy Bentham, who had already proposed utility as a basis for moral and political philosophy. It was a dozen years later that he came to know and occasionally refer to Bentham, James Mill, and the British utilitarian school, or Philosophical Radicals. The importance of utility for Say was in its impact on the theory of value, of value in the economic sense, and hence arcane discussions in which the present editor is quite unable to take part. Utility offered an alternative to the earlier labor theory of value, or belief that the value of an object was determined by the amount of human exertion that had gone into its production, a belief shared by the earlier classical economists, and later by Karl Marx and ensuing Marxists. The discussion of "utility" occurs near the beginning of Say's *Treatise* of 1803, on page 24 of the first volume. Significantly, it is advanced to page 3 of the second edition, and hence to the very beginning of the English translation made from the fourth edition of 1819.

Here is what Say said on utility in 1803, with allusion to the physics of his time:

> . . . The mass of matter of which the world is composed is never increased or diminished. Not an atom is lost, and not a single new atom is created. Things then are not *produced*, but only reproduced in other forms, and what we call production is in fact only a *reproduction*.

I sow a grain of wheat, and it produces twenty. It does not draw them from nothing; it initiates an operation of nature by which different substances formerly in the earth, in water, and in air are changed into grains of wheat. These different substances were of no use while separated; they acquired a use by becoming grains of wheat.

This indicates how the word *production* is to be understood throughout this book. *Production* is not *creation*; it is the production of utility.

Production, or reproduction if you like, not being the production of matter, but only the production of utility, is not to be measured by the length, volume, or weight of a product but only by its degree of utility.

For an exact measure of production we would then need an exact measure of the utility of each thing. But how to measure utility? What seems necessary for one person may seem entirely superfluous to another.

Nevertheless, whatever variety there may be in the tastes and needs of men, they arrive among themselves at a general estimate of the utility of a particular object, an estimate that they reach by considering the quantity of other objects that they would agree to give in exchange for the object in question.

I may judge, for example, that the utility of a coat is three times that of a hat, if I find that in general others agree to give me three hats in exchange for a coat.

And if, for greater convenience, we observe the quantity of one product, for example of such coins as the *écu*, that will be given in exchange for each of two other objects, we can form an idea of the proportion existing between the exchange value of one of these two objects and the value of the other.

Thus I would say that a quantity of wheat that can be exchanged, or sold, for a hundred *écus* is a product equal in value to a quantity of linen cloth obtainable for a hundred *écus*. I could say that a meter of linen cloth that can be sold for 30 francs is a product worth twenty times as much as wrapping cloth that could be sold for 30 sous [since there were twenty sous in the franc].

I here employ a valuation in money, because money is the most convenient and widely used, but the estimate of exchange value could be made in terms of any other product. The estimate in money is itself subject to many inexactitudes, as the reader will see later in my book [in a hundred pages devoted to money]. But it suffices, nevertheless, for most cases with which Political Economy is concerned. . . .

He continues by applying the concept of utility to various kinds of "industry." This word, in this preindustrial age, could mean any productive activity in which people were industriously at work. He also takes issue with his predecessors the Physiocrats, disparagingly known as "economists," who held that land (that is, the material environment) was the only real source of wealth, and work upon land the only truly productive activity, as in mining or most especially in agriculture.

From the preceding we can explain how various industries, although they draw nothing out of nothingness, can yet yield *products*, and how manufacturing industry and commercial industry are productive in precisely the same sense as agricultural industry. They give value to raw materials or enhance an already existing value. And what does agriculture do, except that, with the aid of a strong tool, it gives value to forms of matter already existing in nature?

It is from misunderstanding this principle that the sect of *Economists*, who indeed included some very enlightened writers, fell into serious errors. *Raw materials* and *wealth* were for them synonymous; and agricultural industry, being the only one that drew raw materials from the hands of nature, was for them the only one that produced wealth. The *Economists* did not realize that wealth consists not in any material but in the value of the material; that a material when rendered suitable for use signifies much more wealth than raw material; and that a man who has a quintal of woollen fabrics and fine cloth in his storehouse is much richer than a man who has a quintal of raw wool.

Commercial industry is as productive as manufacturing industry because it heightens the value of a product by transporting it from one place to another. It is a way of making things useful which otherwise would not be, a procedure no less useful, no less complex, and no less hazardous than in the other two industries. . . .

He goes on to apply the conception of utility to consumption, in which utility is lost.

People cannot make use of products without destroying them; thus food when it is eaten, or a coat when it is entirely worn out, have ceased to exist. This destruction is called *consumption*.

As production is not creation but only production of utility, so *consumption* is not *destruction* but only a *destruction of utility*, which brings on a *destruction of value*. We can no more annihilate a thing than create it; but we can reduce it to the point of its having no more use and hence no more value for human beings.

The *consumer* is the last person through whose hands a product passes, the one who uses and *consumes* it. Thus we say *consume*, not only of things that we eat, but of those that give us clothing and pleasures, of everything, in a word, whose value is diminished however slightly by use. Silver buckles are consumed like a hat or a dinner, although more slowly.

These ideas on production and consumption enter into Say's discussion of "immaterial products," or what are now called services, and into a critical comment on Adam Smith. We assume that in the following example the prescribed medicine was a physical object (not a "service") procured from a pharmacist.

A doctor comes to visit a sick person, observes his symptoms, prescribes a remedy, and departs without leaving a product that the sick person or his family can transmit to others or even preserve for their own future consumption.

Was the industry of the doctor unproductive? Who would think so? The sick person has been helped. Was this production unsusceptible to exchange? Not at all, since the doctor's advice has been paid for. But the need for the advice disappeared as soon as it was given. The product was in the speaking, the consumption was in the hearing. It was consumed at the same time as it was given.

This is what I call an *immaterial product*.

The industry of a musician or actor yields a product of the same kind. It gives you a pleasure which it is impossible to preserve, to retain for later consumption, or to use in exchange for other enjoyments. It has its price, but it does not last beyond the moment of its production, except possibly as a memory.

The famous Adam Smith refused to give the results of such industries the name of *products*. He called the labor involved in them *unproductive*. This followed from the meaning he attached to the word wealth. Instead of making wealth mean anything having an exchange value, he used it only for things having an exchange value *susceptible to preservation*, and hence denied it to products consumed at the moment of their creation.

Yet the industry of a medical doctor, or, to take other examples, of a government administrator, a lawyer or a judge, is of the same kind and satisfies needs that are so necessary that no society could subsist without their labors. Are the fruits of such labor unreal? They are so real that they are obtained at the price of some material product to which Smith accords the name of wealth, and so real that by repeated exchanges the producers of immaterial products acquire fortunes.

To descend to things of pure enjoyment, there is no doubt that the performance of a stage play gives as much pleasure as a pound of chocolates or a piece of fireworks, which in Smith's doctrine are called products. It seems unreasonable to me to claim that the talent of a painter is productive, but of a musician is not. . . .

From the nature of immaterial products it follows that they cannot be accumulated, and do nothing to augment the national capital. A nation having a crowd of musicians, priests, and government employees might be a nation well entertained, well indoctrinated, and well governed. But that would be all. Its capital would receive no direct growth from the labor of these industrious men.

Consequently, nothing is done for the public prosperity when means are found to make the labor of one of these occupations more necessary. To increase labor of this kind is simultaneously to increase consumption. When this consumption is an enjoyment there is some consolation, but when it is a bad thing we must agree that such a system is to be deplored.

This is what happens everywhere when legislation is complicated. The labor of lawyers, becoming more considerable and more difficult, occupies more people and is more highly paid. What is gained? Are rights better defended? Surely not: the complication of laws rather promotes bad faith by providing new subterfuges, while adding almost nothing to the solidity of a good legal system. Litigation becomes more frequent and lengthy, which may be good for some, but which the sane majority of the public will always regard as an evil, even when they have won their case.

It is therefore impossible to agree with Garnier [the French translator and annotator of Adam Smith] in his conclusion that since the labor of physicians, lawyers, and such persons is productive it can be multiplied like any other labor to the national advantage. But the case is the same as if we were to multiply manual labor on a product in order to produce it. Productive labor on immaterial products is productive only so far as the product is useful. Beyond that point, it is purely unproductive labor.

To complicate the laws for them to be unscrambled by lawyers is like making oneself ill in order to need a doctor.

But ignoring the amplifications and refinements of these and other ideas in Say's thousand pages, let us turn to the word "entrepreneur." The historical dictionaries of both the French and English languages cite J.-B. Say as the first to use this word in its modern economic sense. In the nineteenth century it occurred in English as a foreign expression, printed in italics, to designate the person who initiated or financed a theatrical production. Since *entreprendre* in French means simply to undertake, an *entrepreneur* is an undertaker, a word obviously unusable for the intended purpose. Say's English translation of 1821 renders *entrepreneur* as "adventurer," which to a modern reader suggests the merchant adventurers of the sixteenth century or the venture capitalists of the twentieth. It was an awkward translation, as the translator admitted in a footnote. It is only in the latter half of the twentieth century that "entrepreneur" has become common in Anglo-American usage.

In discussing slavery, as shown above, Say had found five categories of persons involved in production, one of them the slave; but since slavery was irrelevant in most contexts, and was in any case a form of labor, there were basically only four categories: the persons who could provide capital, knowledge, labor, and enterprise. Say often called the latter the *entrepreneur d'industrie*, but since *industrie* could mean any productive activity it can usually be omitted without loss in translation. The role of the *entrepreneur* was to assemble what the other three categories had to contribute. He combined the inputs of capital, knowledge, and labor to launch and manage an enterprise. He might possess some of the needed capital and knowledge himself, and he certainly worked, as did his employed labor; the problem was to distinguish what he earned in the role of entrepreneur.

THE PROFITS OF THE ENTREPRENEUR

The question in this chapter is to determine only that portion of the income of an entrepreneur that can be regarded as compensation for his work. If the head of an enterprise owns a portion of the capital used in the operation I put him for that portion in the class of capitalists, and the portion of income that he so receives is part of the income on the capital employed.

At this point Say has a footnote criticizing Adam Smith, who, he says, confused his own arguments by failing to distinguish between the "profits" of the entrepreneur and the "profits of stock" (Smith's word for "capital").

It is rare that someone receiving compensation as an entrepreneur does not also receive some interest on capital. It is rare for the head of an enterprise to have borrowed from others the total capital that he is using. If he has purchased tools by drawing on his own capital, or made advances from his own resources, he receives some of his income as an entrepreneur and some of it as a capitalist.

We are reminded again that we are in an early stage of the Industrial Revolution; the apparatus used is called "tools" (*ustensiles*), and the capital is not raised by issue of bonds or shares of stock. And a farmer may be an entrepreneur as well as someone in manufacturing or commerce.

It is the compensation of these entrepreneurs that we wish to examine. It is regulated like the price of all other things by the relationship between the *quantity of demand* for this kind of work and the quantity available for circulation, that is, the *quantity of supply*. This latter quantity is limited by two principal causes, which keep the price for this kind of work at a high level.

It is usually the entrepreneur who must find the funds needed for his project. I do not draw the consequence that he must be rich, for he can carry on his operation with borrowed funds. But he must at least be solvent, known as a man of prudence, probity, and order, and hence by the nature of his connections be able to obtain the capital that he himself does not possess.

These conditions exclude many people from the competition.

The other "principal cause" limiting the supply of entrepreneurs was the requirement of knowledge. Here we detect an ambiguity: the entrepreneur might bring in the knowledge of scientists and experts to give it practical application, but he also needed a knowledge of entrepreneurship itself, and it is this kind of knowledge that Say describes.

Secondly, this kind of work requires judgment and knowledge. Judgment, especially when it must extend to comparing opportunities in distant places, is a fairly rare gift, so that only a limited number of men can provide work of this kind.

Those who, by presumption, undertake this kind of work without sufficient ability make products whose value does not pay for the costs of production, and so does not pay enough for their own labor and the interest on their funds. Sometimes, indeed, far from being able to remunerate their own efforts from the value of the product, they are obliged to provide the wages of their workers and the interest on capital from their own pockets. Matters cannot long continue in this way, and their own labor will soon go out of circulation. Those left will be the ones who can continue with success, that is, with the needed ability. In this way the requirement of ability restricts the number who can provide the work of the entrepreneur.

Not all kinds of industry require in those who undertake them the same amount of ability and knowledge. A farmer who is an agricultural entrepreneur need not know as many things as a merchant dealing with distant places. As long as the farmer is familiar with the routine methods involving two or three crops, from which he derives his income, he can come off successfully. The kinds of knowledge needed for carrying on a long-continuing trade are of a higher order. It is necessary to know not only the nature and qualities of the goods on which one is speculating, but also to form an idea of the needs and markets in places where one expects to sell them. Hence the entrepreneur must keep constantly informed of the price of each of these goods in different parts of the world. To judge these prices accurately he must have knowledge of various currencies and their relative values, or what is called foreign exchange. He must know something about means of transportation and must measure the risks and the costs that they impose; the laws and us-ages of peoples with whom he is dealing; and enough knowledge of men not to be deceived in the confidence he puts in them, the missions he charges them with, and any other relationships that may arise. If the knowledge that makes a good farmer is more common than the knowledge that makes a good merchant it is not surprising that the labors of the former are less well rewarded than those of the latter.

This is not to say that all branches of commercial industry require rarer qualities than does agricultural industry. A retail merchant may carry on his occupation by routine, like most farmers, while some kinds of agriculture require sagacity and pains that are far from common. It is for the reader to make the application in particular cases. . . .

We shall see, in speaking of the profits of the worker, what advantage the head of an enterprise has over the worker because of their respective positions. It is enough here to note other advantages from which the head of an enterprise can benefit if he is astute. He is the intermediary between the capitalist and the landowner, between the man of science and the worker, between all classes of producers and between them and consumers. He manages the work of production, is at the center of several interrelationships, and profits from what others know or what they do not know and from unforeseen developments in the course of production. So it is in this class of producers, when events are favorable and reinforce their abilities, that almost all the largest fortunes are made.

Implicit here, though the word occurs only once incidentally, is the idea of risk. In his later writings Say put a clearer emphasis on this element in the entrepreneur's role. More than the others engaged in production the entrepreneur had to deal, day by day, with uncertainties in both the present and the future; he might make mistakes, and sustain losses instead of gains. A good example of Say's mature thinking on this matter is found in some commentaries he made on a book by the Russian economist Heinrich Storch, published in French at St. Petersburg in 1815 for instruction of the grand dukes of Russia, and again at Paris in 1823.

M. Storch is far from giving the importance that he should to the functions of the entrepreneur.

The entrepreneur, whether in agriculture, manufacturing or commerce, is the one who at his own risk and peril undertakes to supply society with the products it needs. He estimates the costs of production that his product requires, and judges in advance its value when produced; he assembles all the elements in an enterprise, and sets up its management and procedures. Since he must perpetually make purchases and sales, and reach all kinds of agreements, he must have a knowledge of men and affairs, evaluate risks, foresee the vicissitudes of trade and the influence of war and peace and bad laws. The combination of qualities and talents needed to make an industrial enterprise prosper [in the now obsolete sense of "industrial"], or even to sustain it, creates a kind of monopoly in favor of men who are able to conceive, form, and conduct such an enterprise. Those who are lacking in prudence and understanding cannot long compete with those who have them. Such are the causes that establish, for entrepreneurs, the profits that are independent of their capital, and are much higher than the salary even of a high-level employee, who runs no risk on his own account, collects his salary whatever happens, and hazards neither his own funds nor his reputation in case of bad fortune.

Say's chapter on the "profits of the entrepreneur" in the *Treatise* of 1803 is followed by one on "the profits of the worker," which precedes the one on "the profits of the slave" as quoted in the last chapter. In his comments on slavery he said that the worker, as distinguished from the slave, had a free choice of employment, or of the kind of work that he wanted to do. He remarked elsewhere that subsistence, or the minimum level below which wages could not fall, might mean more than the barest subsistence, that it might be culturally determined, that, as he put it, the French worker must have his wine and the English worker his beer. But he was well aware that workers in general had little free choice of employment, and that most of them lived in poverty.

THE PROFITS OF THE WORKER

. . . Independently of the reasons given in this and preceding chapters, explaining why the income of an entrepreneur (even when he receives no income as a capitalist) is in general higher than that of a simple worker, there are other reasons, doubtless less legitimate fundamentally, whose effect must not be misunderstood.

The wages of the worker are determined adversarially by agreement between the worker and the head of an industry. The former tries to receive the most possible, and the latter to give the least, but in this kind of negotiation the employer enjoys an advantage quite apart from those given by the nature of his functions. The employer and the worker have an equal need of each other, since neither can earn an income without the other's aid, but the need of the employer is less immediate and less pressing. There are few employers who cannot live for several months, or even several years, without employing a single worker, but there are few workers who can remain unemployed for several weeks without being reduced to the utmost extremity. It is indeed hard for this difference in their position not to affect the settlement of their wages.

It is also easier for employers to reach agreements with one another to keep wages down than for workers to do so to make them high. The employers are less numerous and can more easily communicate among themselves. The workers, on the other hand, can hardly come to agreements without their leagues having the appearance of revolt, which the civil authorities will always hasten to put down.

These "leagues" were the shadowy, transitory and barely tolerated organizations that preceded the formation of labor unions. Say at this point says nothing for or against them except in connection with foreign trade.

> A system that bases the principal gains of a nation on exportation of its products even considers these leagues of workers to be harmful to the prosperity of the state, since they bring on a rise of prices for merchandise for export, with damage to the desired advantage in foreign markets. But what is a prosperity that consists in keeping a numerous class in one's own country in poverty, to give lower prices to foreigners, who profit from privations you have imposed upon yourself!

No hostility is expressed to an organized labor that might deal responsibly with employers in the best interests of both, since they depended on each other.

On what has been called Say's Law much has been written by economists. Here again the present editor can do no more than select what seem to be relevant passages. Known also as the law of markets, Say's Law holds that in the long run supply and demand must be in balance. There can be no overproduction in a general sense. In a simplified popular form, it holds that "supply creates demand." This may seem somewhat contrary to common sense, which might suppose that demand for a product is what induces someone to supply it, and in any case is contrary to ideas associated with John Maynard Keynes, in which a stimulus to demand will increase supply—for example, that payment of welfare benefits to the unemployed will enable them to purchase goods and so restore business activity and employment.

The "law" seems to be touched on only marginally in the *Treatise* of 1803. In the following excerpt the "means of production" means the assemblage of capital, knowledge, and labor available to produce, that is, the supply side of the potential equation. Say's argument is that if such means are excessive for one product they should be transferred to producing another. As usual in this book the italics are his:

> *The extent of demand for means of production in general* does not depend, as too many have imagined, on the *extent of consumption*. Consumption is not a cause; it is an effect. To consume, one must buy; but one can buy only with what one has produced. . . .
>
> *But,* someone will say, *if there is merchandise that cannot be sold there must necessarily be more means of production employed than there are ca-*

pabilities for consuming the products. Not at all; overproduction occurs only when too many means of production are applied to one kind of production and not enough to another. What does a shortage of sales really mean? It means the difficulty in obtaining some other merchandise (in goods or money) in exchange for what one offers. The means of production are insufficient for the former while they are superabundant for the latter. A region within a country may be unable to sell all its grain, but if a manufacture is established there, and part of the funds and industry formerly devoted to agriculture are devoted to another kind of production, the products of both taken together will find an outlet without difficulty, although the amount of products has increased rather than diminished. Shortage of sales thus comes not from superabundance but from a defective use of the means of production.

Garnier, in the notes he joins to his excellent translation of Adam Smith, says that in the old nations of Europe, where capital has accumulated for centuries, a superabundance of annual product *would be an obstruction to circulation if it were not absorbed by a proportionate consumption.* I can see that circulation can be obstructed by superabundance of certain products, but that can only be a passing evil, for people will soon cease to engage in a line of production whose products exceed the need for them and lose their value, and they will turn to the production of goods more in demand. But I do not see how the products of a nation in general can ever be too abundant, for each such product [through payment of wages, profits, etc.] provides the means for purchasing another. The mass of products composes the mass of a nation's wealth, and wealth is no more inconvenient to nations than it is to private persons.

It can be seen here that Say's argument rests on a belief in a more easy mobility of labor and a more prompt fluidity of capital than might occur in real life, so that the consequences of overproduction in a given commodity, though transitory, might be unacceptable to those involved. This was apparent to contemporaries, one of whom was the Swiss economist J. C. Sismondi. Say replied to Sismondi much later, in 1824, in an article in the *Revue encyclopédique* entitled "On the balance of consumption and production."

> In the number before last of the *Revue encyclopédique* M. Sismondi published an article on the *balance of consumption and production* in which that estimable writer restates the fears he had already expressed elsewhere, fears that the progress of the practical arts [as in science, invention, and labor-saving machines] would multiply products to the point of making their complete sale impossible, and so bring distress upon many producers, especially among the working class.

This doctrine contradicts what David Ricardo and I have tried to establish in our writings, where we say that products are exchanged for other products, and that their multiplication can only multiply human enjoyments and increase the population of states. . . .

In a very broad view of human societies we see them as anthills in which individuals move in all directions to obtain what meets their needs and desires. The more they move and extend their searches, the more they provide themselves with things that are necessary or simply pleasant to have. . . . But while each anthill in our woods works for a single storehouse, in the interest of its small republic, each person in our human anthills works only on one kind of the useful things called *products*, and procures by exchange all other things that he needs, for to sell what one produces in order to buy what one wants to consume is to exchange what one makes or does for the things one needs.

From this, it is clearly possible for a particular thing to be produced in a greater quantity than what is needed. If in a society composed of ten thousand families five thousand engaged in making crockery vases, and five thousand in making shoes, this society would undeniably have too many vases and too many shoes, and would lack many things no less favorable to its well-being. But it is also evident that this inconvenience would arise not from producing too much, but from not producing exactly what is wanted.

But if it be objected that a human society, using human intelligence and the means available from nature and the practical arts, can produce . . . more than the same society can consume, I would ask how it happens that we know of no society that is completely provided for, since even in the so-called most flourishing societies seven-eighths of the population lacks many products regarded as necessary, not merely for an opulent family but for a modest household. I live at this moment in one of the richest regions of France. Yet of twenty houses there are nineteen in which, on entering them, I see none but the coarsest food, nothing to serve the well-being of families, none of the things that the English call *comfortable*; not enough beds for all members of the family to lie on; not enough furniture for them to sit at ease for their meals; not enough linen, nor of soap, for proper laundering, etc.

He goes on to argue at some length that the alleviation of such poverty must come from further use of the "arts," that is, from science and invention and reduction of the costs of production, by which productivity is enhanced so that the worker receives a higher wage with which to acquire more goods at lower prices. And so far as this does not happen he puts the blame on those whose crucial role he had defined and emphasized, namely, the entrepreneurs.

What M. de Sismondi fears above all is overproduction, which closes down manufactures, interrupts commerce, and leaves workers without employment. But this overproduction, when it occurs, is the consequence of miscalculation by entrepreneurs, that is, of an industry not sufficiently advanced and enlightened. If the heads of an enterprise in agriculture, manufacturing, or commerce knew how to create products suited to their consumers, if they knew how to set prices facilitating consumption, and if consumers for their part were industrious enough to offer something in exchange, this overproduction would end, and would result in new means of prosperity.

Overproduction is always unintended; it is brought on by the entrepreneurs. In any kind of industry it is the entrepreneur and not the workers who decides what is to be produced, and in what quantity. The interest of the entrepreneur, always and everywhere, is to conform to the needs of a country; otherwise the sales value of a product would fall below its cost of production, and the entrepreneur would lose. His interest guarantees that for each product the quantity created cannot permanently exceed needs . . . that arise from the greater ease of life and more civilized tastes that follow from a more active industry and less costly production. Coarse food, clothing, and housing always go with a deficiency in activity and industry. . . .

Say rejects Sismondi's idea that governments may sometimes have to intervene to protect workers:

There are great dangers in accepting maxims contrary to what I have said. They persuade the public authorities that they can, without destroying industry, and even while protecting it, have a role in the nature of products and the mode of their production, and interpose between the employer and the worker to regulate their respective interests. Why does M. Sismondi say that *it is the task of the legislator to reconcile the interests of those who take part in the same act of production, instead of putting them in opposition?* As if the whole economy of a society did not turn on the debate of such interests among themselves! Why does he wish to examine the question of *laws that might require the employer to guarantee the subsistence of the worker he employs?* Such an examination would paralyze the spirit of enterprise. The mere fear that public power might intervene in private agreements is a scourge that damages the prosperity of a nation. . . .

Nothing is more dangerous than views that lead to regulation of the use made of properties. To do so is as bold as trying to regulate the innocent use that a man might make of his own hands and faculties, which are also a form of property. If the authorities can require an employer to pay a certain wage, they can require the worker to perform a certain labor. With such a system slavery reappears; it violates the prop-

erty of the poor man, which is his labor, more than it violates the property of the entrepreneur, who can employ his capital according to his
talents and endlessly varying circumstances.

We have here a declaration of *laissez-faire*, a French term that Say did
not use but was later appropriated by Anglophone commentators on the
free-market economy. Say, as has been seen, was well aware of the disadvantages of the worker in negotiation with an employer, but he put his
hopes for permanent improvement in the worker's lot in the new science
of political economy, by which capital, labor, and knowledge could all
become more productive for the good of all concerned.

A similar faith in political economy entered into his discussion of
problems of population. On this matter Say was less innovative; he himself was aware of many others who had addressed the subject throughout the eighteenth century, although he had not yet seen Malthus's
work on population, of which the first edition had appeared in 1798.
Malthus there took issue with various writers including the French revolutionary Condorcet, who, in his *Progress of the Human Mind* (published posthumously in 1795), had portrayed science and enlightenment
as causes of boundless advancement in the future. According to
Malthus, such optimism was mistaken; population would grow at a geo-
metric rate while the means of subsistence could grow only arithmeti-
cally; if the wages and living standards of the workers should rise there
could be no corresponding increase in food supply; the workers would
only produce more children, some of whom would die of malnutrition
and others, as adults, would be so numerous as to depress wages to their
previous level.

Say agreed that the size of a population must always be proportionate
to its productive capacity. But, as he saw it, it was not a question of the
production only of food. A people could produce other goods and services, in indefinite amount, which by exchange could be used to obtain
subsistence for all, and more than subsistence for most. Relying like
Condorcet on the progress of the human mind, Say therefore shared in
Condorcet's confidence in the future. Malthus himself modified his
views in his later writings. Say, in stressing productivity as the safeguard
against overpopulation and poverty, anticipated ideas that later became
common in both economics and demography. His political economy
was no dismal science, and it taught no iron law of wages.

He included a whole chapter entitled "On Production in Its Relation
to Population" in his *Treatise* of 1803:

> . . . By means of exchange and commerce the production of goods
> for housing and clothing may in truth substitute for the production of
> food. The Dutch obtain wheat by the sale of their cloth, and North
> America obtains sugar and coffee in exchange for sending pre-cut lum-

ber to build houses in the Antilles. Even immaterial products ["ser-vices"], though they cannot be transported, can add to the food supply of a nation. The money received from a foreigner who pays to consult someone famous in the practical or liberal arts can be sent back abroad to purchase more substantial goods. Thus a product meant to satisfy one kind of need can satisfy another. . . .

If population is limited only by the impossibility of meeting the needs of a larger number of people, and if products of whatever kind will satisfy needs of another kind, it follows that population will always be in proportion to the quantity of products.

Doubtless in a country where fortunes are very unequally distributed, or where dissolute moral habits [echoes from *Olbia*!] enable a few indi-viduals to consume a quantity of products that would support a multi-tude—such a country, I say, cannot maintain as large a population as a more sober country with the same quantity of products; but all things being equal, the population of a country is in proportion to its prod-ucts. This is a truth recognized by most writers on Political Economy, however various their opinions on other matters.

Here he has a footnote citing, with exact page references, the books of sixteen French and British writers, not including Malthus's *Essay on the Principles of Population* of 1798, which clearly had not yet come to his attention by 1803.

It seems to me that the perfectly natural consequence has not been seen, that is, that nothing except what favors production could promote a growth of population, and that nothing could permanently diminish population except what undermines the sources of production. . . .

He argues that losses due to famine and epidemics are eventually made up, and that the efforts of governments to increase population by merely passing laws have been unsuccessful.

What really encourages population is active industry. In industrious countries population multiplies rapidly, and when a virgin soil is com-bined with the activity of a whole nation that tolerates no idlers the growth of population is astonishing, as in the United States where it doubles every twenty years. . . .

Another consequence of the preceding is that the inhabitants of a country are no less well provided with the necessities of life when their number increases, nor better provided when their number declines. Their fate depends on the quantity of products that they have at their disposal, and these can be abundant for a numerous population, or scarce for a small one. Shortage was more common in Europe in the middle ages than in recent times when the population is obviously much greater. England was not as well provided for in the time of Queen Elizabeth as it is today, though it then had only half as many inhabitants; and the people of Spain, reduced now to eight million souls, live in less comfort than when they numbered twenty-four millions.

It all seems to be a corollary of Say's Law: products are acquired by other products, in a long-run aggregate balance. In any case, and whatever constructive ideas might be found in the first edition of Say 's *Treatise on Political Economy*, Napoleon Bonaparte did not like the book, and its message could not be made widely known.

But as Say withdrew into private life he was able to practice what he could not preach. He became an entrepreneur himself. He assembled and managed the factors in production. To obtain capital he added to whatever he had by joining with a silent partner whose name is unfortunately not recorded, and for a factory building he acquired from the government a large and vacant Benedictine abbey that had been confiscated during the Revolution. (He thus illustrated an important point, how the revolutionary nationalization of church properties contributed to French economic development.) He obtained knowledge by preliminary study at the Conservatory of Arts and Trades, whose usefulness he had praised a few years before in the *Décade philosophique*. By this time, in 1804, he had already begun to recruit labor, for we are told by his son that he worked at the Conservatory with two others described as his *contremaîtres*, or foremen. Together they examined the recently improved machines for spinning cotton, some of them brought surreptitiously from England. From observing the machines as exhibited, and from demonstrators employed by the Conservatory who explained them, they learned how they were built, how they worked, and how they should be maintained and repaired.

The old abbey, with an adjoining village and stream of running water, was located in the department of Pas-de-Calais at the northern tip of France. It needed rehabilitation, and in any case its rooms had to be rearranged to convert them into a manufacturing establishment. Say's machines ran by water power (not steam engines), so that he had to build water mills, and as the years passed he added a few new buildings to the abbey. He himself trained many of the villagers to be laborers in his plant. By 1810 he employed 400 workers and was spinning 100 kilograms of cotton thread a day.

It must be remembered that the British naval blockade, during the Napoleonic wars, was not an attempt to keep British manufactures out of France so much as an effort to destroy the export of French manufactures, and so weaken the French according to older mercantilist ideas. French manufacturers agitated for tariff protection, and even for a prohibition on the importation of cotton threads and yarns, in whose production the British at this time so manifestly excelled. In 1809 the French government ordered a number of its departmental prefects to consult with cotton manufacturers in their departments and make recommendations for action. The prefect of the Pas-de-Calais did so, and found that every cotton spinner in his department favored a protective tariff on cotton thread, with one exception, J.-B. Say. In his report to Paris the prefect enclosed a copy of a letter he had received from Say. In it Say, though a cotton spinner himself who would benefit from the exclusion of imported thread, explained how a tax on it would damage other lines of business. In particular, the finest threads, which France could not yet produce, should be lightly taxed, if at all. He also urged abolition of the existing tax on imports of raw cotton, all of which, of course, had to be imported. A few words of the letter are worth quoting, for they repeat the "doctrine" in the *Treatise*.

> . . . If the introduction of foreign thread should be prohibited some of our manufactures would suffer because our French spinners cannot at present produce thread of the finest quality. . . . [Those suffering would be] the manufactures of muslins, cambrics, and quilted and knitted goods which are all made with foreign threads.
>
> But a measure that would be simultaneously favorable to all branches of cotton manufacture and to all consumers, as well as unfavorable to sales by foreign producers, would be to abolish the impolitic duty levied on the introduction of raw cotton into France, which is now at 66 francs per hundredweight.
>
> This abolition, by which the government would lose very little, would be favorable to all kinds of manufacture because without this tax the spinner could give a lower price to the weaver, the weaver to the producer of printed cloth, and the cloth printer to the consumer. With the price of all these articles lower, the foreign spinner, weaver, and printer, and the dealers in damask, cambrics, etc. on the other side of the Channel, would be so much the less able to compete with our manufacturers.
>
> What the government would gain in higher taxes paid by these industries would make up for the small loss in revenue from import duties.

Napoleon's government, nevertheless, with its perpetual war costs, not only maintained its import duties on cotton threads and fabrics but substantially raised the duty on raw cotton in 1812. Say, apparently thinking that with this added burden the future of his enterprise was threatened, sold out to his partner and returned to Paris in 1813. We have no information on how much he sold it for, but we know from a letter he wrote to Thomas Jefferson in 1814 that he had a sum of 60,000 francs at his disposal.

With the year 1814 everything was reversed. The wars seemed to be over; the Russian, Prussian, and Austrian armies entered Paris in March, Napoleon abdicated in April, and by June the second edition of Say's *Treatise* was in print. But a France under a restored Bourbon king, supported by returned émigrés and jubilant royalists, was not a country in which an old republican like Say could see an agreeable future. In his uncertainty he turned to two incongruous personages, the tsar of Russia and the ex-president of the United States.

Alexander I of Russia was generally known, and feared by his own allies, for his liberal and constitutionalist sympathies. Say had reason to think that his new book, though now in print, might be suppressed as it had been in 1803. As he told Jefferson, he therefore put it under the protection, or *sauvegarde*, of the Russian tsar. We find on the next page after its title page a dedication "To his Majesty Alexander I, Emperor of all the Russias," and then:

Sire:

Your Imperial Majesty has allowed me to place at his feet this fruit of my studies and labors. For ten years I have been obliged to hide, as if it were a crime, a work that seems to me to offer some useful findings to Princes and Nations. But at last the power of your armies, Sire, supported by the efforts of your generous allies and the fervor of all friends of enlightenment in Europe, has broken the chains binding all liberal thought, and overthrown the barbarism that we were terrified to see making such rapid progress. . . .

Say's correspondence with Jefferson illuminates many points already made. We must go back to 1803, when he had sent a copy of the first edition of the *Treatise* to Jefferson, addressing him as President of the United States, and conveying both his personal compliments and a belief that the United States might become the light of the world.

Please accept the homage of my *Treatise on Political Economy* as a mark of my high regard for your personal qualities and the principles that you profess. I hope you may find in it some signs of that enlightened love of liberty and humanity for which right-thinking men so much respect you.

The happiness enjoyed by your country, and greatly enhanced under your administration, is enough to arouse the envy of the nations of Europe; your prosperity may be the source of theirs. They will see the degree of happiness attainable by a human society that practices common sense in its legislation, economy in its expenditures, and morality in its politics. It will no longer be possible to represent wise counsels as mere impractical theories.

It is for you also to show the friends of liberty in Europe how personal freedom is compatible with maintenance of the social body. The finest cause will no longer be soiled by excesses, and it will be seen that civil liberty is the true aim of social organization and that political liberty must be a means to this end.

The United States are the children of Europe, and more worthy than their fathers. We are aged parents brought up in foolish prejudices, bound by old obstacles, and subjected to many puerile ideas. You will show us the true means of our liberation. You have done more than conquer your freedom; you have affirmed it.

Jefferson responded cordially but briefly in 1804. He had been reading Malthus's gloomy thoughts on population growth, he told Say; he wondered whether America and Europe might reach an agreed upon division of labor, in which America with its vast and yet uncultivated land could in the future feed both itself and a growing population of Europeans, "who in return would send us in exchange our clothes and other comforts"; but he offered this thought only as a matter for further inquiry.

Say wrote again to Jefferson ten years later, in June 1814, sending a copy of the second edition of his *Treatise*. He explains the history of the book, his present uncertainties, his reliance on the tsar Alexander, and his thoughts of emigrating to the United States.

Monsieur:

Ten years ago I had the honor of receiving your letter of February 1, 1804, acknowledging receipt of the first edition of my *Treatise on Political Economy*. . . .

For ten years I have wrapped myself in obscurity to avoid the sad impact of a savage tyranny that has set back France for several centuries, but having a numerous family and lacking the means to live without lucrative work I established a cotton manufactory about fifty leagues from Paris, which prospered until I was forced to give up my business by the excessive taxes imposed by the government, and by a general impoverishment that almost destroyed all consumption.

Moments of leisure in a busy life in the depths of the countryside allowed me to start over and entirely remake my *Treatise on Political Economy*, and the latest political events have finally removed the obstacles to the printing of my work. It has now just appeared, and to prevent the stopping of its circulation I have put it under the protection of the emperor of Russia. Freedom of the press exists only in our public proclamations; in reality there is none, and authors are allowed only to prove that the government is right whatever it does.

Such is a succinct history of the book of which I take the liberty of sending you a copy, as my homage to your virtues and your enlightened views. Please accept it, Monsieur, with your customary indulgence. If you take the trouble to look through it, I flatter myself to think that you will find that I have been able, by a better method, to place Political Economy on such a secure foundation that it will henceforth be counted among the positive sciences. I do not think that it can now face any insoluble difficulty, and the consequences to be drawn from it for improvement of the social art and for human happiness seem to me immense.

My son, a young man of twenty, sent to the United States as supercargo by a well-established commercial house at Nantes, has had to make the trip by land last April from Charleston to New York. Mr. Warden, your consul-general in France, has kindly given him a letter of introduction to you, Monsieur, and if he has not had to change his plans he will be paying his respects to you. It is possible that the business in which my son is engaged will lead him to set up a commercial establishment in the United States, and I will admit that I am thinking seriously of settling there myself with my wife and four younger children. I would be deterred only by the uncertainty of being able to make a living by using my assets, which are not great, to purchase and develop a tract of land.

In this situation, and feeling the need to breathe the air of a free country, and with nothing but hope that France may be well governed, I would regard it as a great favor on your part if you could be so good as to give me, or have given to me, a reply to the following questions to help in my decision:

Is there, in the neighborhood of Charlottesville in Virginia, land available that is already cleared, or at least partly cleared, and with already enough buildings for both housing and exploitation?

How many acres would be needed for the purchaser who develops it to live with a family of seven or eight persons?

In the designated neighborhood, and with buildings sufficient to live in and begin cultivation at the time of arrival, what would be the cost per acre?

A resolution of these questions would allow me to make a judgment and take action.

I specify the neighborhood of Charlottesville because it is neither so close to the seaports as to make the land too expensive, nor so distant as to present the first rigors of a new settlement. Its middle latitude preserves it from both the stinging cold of Northern states and the stifling heat of those in the South. I have no other ground of preference, nor any objection to any other locality having the same advantages. Other things being equal, the more inhabited regions would serve me best, for I do not flee from men but only from the men of old Europe who are shallow and corrupt. In any case, at my age, which is 47, I know that in seeking men I should not hope to find angels. . . .

There are some strange silences in this letter. He seems not to know that if he were to settle near Charlottesville he would be one of Jefferson's neighbors. And he seems not to have realized that if he were to own a plantation in Virginia he would probably become a slave owner, a role that he could hardly relish, although it is true that it was the West Indian slave owners that had attracted most of his reprobation. One would suppose that with his experience as a cotton spinner he would have preferred to settle in New England, with its incipient industrialization, despite its "stinging cold."

He wrote again to Jefferson in the following August, before enough time had passed for him to receive a reply to his preceding letter, and still pondering the possibility of emigration. He has heard nothing from his son traveling in America, but:

As for myself, if I remain in France, it would be because of the difficulty of moving with a numerous family and only a moderate fortune. I would rather live in a free country, and can hardly flatter myself that this country will become such. Not that the present government is strong enough or intelligent enough to be oppressive, but the people are too uneducated to escape oppression. They imagine in France that they defend their rights by attacking authority, and keep government within proper bounds by being undisciplined, and so the fear of disorders plunges us into servitude. Hence, if with 60,000 francs at my disposal I could become a farmer in your country and subsist comfortably with my family, I think I might so decide. It is for that reason, Monsieur, that I ventured to ask you for information on the present price of land in an inhabited area with the beginnings of enough clearing and building to make possible subsistence during the first year. But I fear I have been indiscreet in discussing my private concerns with you. . . .

With the war of 1812 between the United States and Great Britain still in progress, including a British blockade and an American embargo, Jefferson was delayed in replying to Say until March 1815.

Meanwhile, for Say, the situation radically changed. As it turned out, and partly through the influence of the Russian tsar, France received a constitution that was fairly liberal for its time, and the new regime proved to be more acceptable to Say than he had expected. Someone in the new government, probably after seeing the recently published second edition of the *Treatise*, recommended him for a mission to England to observe the social and economic conditions of that country at the close of the war. Say, therefore, soon after writing his letter of August to Jefferson, spent the next four months on an officially sponsored visit to England in preparation of a report to the French government. Then on March 1, 1815, Napoleon, escaping from Elba, suddenly reappeared in France and proclaimed the restitution of his Empire. During the ensuing three months, remembered as the Hundred Days, various old revolutionaries as well as younger persons who were beginning to be called liberals rallied to Napoleon in the hope of obtaining a liberalized imperial system. One such person, whose name is unknown, but claiming to speak for Napoleon, asked Say to write a paper proving that the French government now under Napoleon was financially more sound and enjoyed a better credit than the British. Say refused; he was writing, or had already written, his report on England for the government of Louis XVIII. He declined the request from Napoleon "to prove what I knew to be false." In his letter to Napoleon's intermediary he observed that, as of April 27, the British government could borrow, that is, sell its bonds, at a rate of 5 percent interest while the French government had to pay almost 9 percent. He concluded the letter by remarking, somewhat insultingly, that "French finances would be in a better position if political economy were a little better understood among us."

It must have been at about this time that Say received the expected reply from Jefferson, dated at Monticello March 2, 1815, almost exactly on the day on which Napoleon had returned to France. Jefferson's letter, running to about twenty-five hundred words, was replete with details of land prices, crop yields, and statistics on the weather. Before answering Say's specific questions on prospects for emigration, he noted the effects of blockade and embargo in the United States:

> . . . We are consequently become manufacturers to a degree incredible to those who do not see it, and who only consider the short period of time during which we have been driven to them by the suicidal policy of England. The prohibiting duties we lay on all articles of foreign manufacture which prudence requires us to establish at home, with the patriotic determination of every good citizen to use no foreign article which can be made within ourselves, without regard to difference of price, secures us against a relapse into foreign dependency. And this cir-

cumstance may be worthy of your consideration, should you continue in the disposition to emigrate to this country. Your manufactory of cotton, on a moderate scale combined with a farm, might be preferable to either singly, and the one or the other might become principal, as experience should recommend. Cotton ready spun is in ready demand, and if woven, still more so.

I will proceed now to answer the inquiries which respect your views of removal; and I am glad that, in looking over our map, your eye has been attracted by the village of Charlottesville, because I am better acquainted with that than any other portion of the United States, being within three or four miles of the place of my birth and residence. It is a portion of country which certainly possesses great advantages, . . . excellently adapted to wheat, maize, and clover; like all mountainous countries it is perfectly healthy, liable to no agues and fevers, or to any particular epidemic, as is evidenced by the robust constitution of its inhabitants, and their numerous families. . . .

There is navigation for boats of six tons from Charlottesville to Richmond, the nearest tidewater, and principal market for our produce. The country is what we call well inhabited, there being in our county, Albemarle, of about seven hundred and fifty square miles, about twenty thousand inhabitants, or twenty-seven to a square mile, of whom, however, one-half are people of color, either slaves or free. The society is much better than is common in country situations; perhaps there is not a better *country* society in the United States. But do not imagine this a Parisian or an academical society. It consists of plain, honest, and rational neighbors, some of them well informed and men of reading, all superintending their farms, hospitable and friendly, and speaking nothing but English. . . .

Most of the hired labor here is of people of color, either slaves or free. An able-bodied man has sixty dollars a year, and is clothed and fed by the employer; a woman half that. White laborers may be had, but they are less subordinate, their wages higher, and their nourishment more expensive. . . .

That it may be for the benefit of your children and their descendants to remove to a country where, for enterprise and talents, so many avenues are open to fortune and fame, I have little doubt. But I should be afraid to affirm that, at your time of life, and with habits formed on the state of society in France, a change for one so entirely different would be for your personal happiness. Fearful, therefore, to persuade, I shall add with sincere truth, that I shall very highly estimate the addition of such a neighbor to our society, and that there is no service within my power which I shall not render with pleasure and promptitude.

It is evident that Jefferson, as if to clarify the silences in Say's letters noted above, thought that he might come as either a planter or a cotton manufacturer, and while welcoming him as a neighbor near Charlottesville called his attention to slavery and expressed doubts on the wisdom of Say's making such a move.

Say never went to America. With Napoleon defeated at Waterloo, and Louis XVIII restored for a second time in 1815, he found the atmosphere in France more suited to his needs. In any case, he must have been too busy in 1815 to consider emigration. He began in that year to give public lectures at a privately organized society called the Athénée, or Athenaeum, and summarized these lectures in a short *Catéchism d'économie politique*, also published in 1815, in which he tried, as he had tried in vain in 1803, to make economic ideas understandable to a wide public. The "catechism" appeared in English in London in 1816 and Philadelphia in 1817, but the English version was never reprinted. Perhaps also as early as 1815 he was already thinking of the next edition of the *Treatise*, of which a third edition came out in 1817. It was soon translated into German, Swedish, Italian, and Spanish, and was followed by a fourth edition which appeared in English in London, Philadelphia, and Boston in 1821. It was also in 1815 that Say published a version of his official report on conditions in England, his *De l'Angeleterre et des Anglais*, with which the next chapter begins.

Chapter Five

THE COMMENTATOR ON ENGLAND

JEAN-BAPTISTE SAY was well qualified to be an observer of England, having lived there for almost two years in his youth, learned the language, and long been an admirer of Adam Smith. His attitude was ambivalent, for he found much to praise and much to condemn. It was an attitude well suited to the time considered in this chapter, from Say's tour of England in 1814 until his death in 1832. The British themselves were ambivalent, or at least divided, in these years on the eve of their Age of Reform, when conservatism was troubled even by liberal Tories and assailed by others like Jeremy Bentham and James Mill who called themselves Philosophical Radicals.

The Britain of 1814 was well advanced in the Industrial Revolution, which was not yet known by that name but was evident in the widespread use of steam engines, the mechanization of textile manufactures, and the growth of cities. It emerged from the wars as the world's chief financial center, having replaced Amsterdam, and as the only important surviving naval and colonial power, having expanded its territory in India and annexed various Dutch and French overseas possessions. Secure in its island, it had been the most persistent adversary of the French since 1793; it had defeated the French with its own army in Spain and Portugal, and used its wealth to subsidize the armies of Prussia, Austria, and Russia. It suffered from serious postwar problems of debt, deficit, inflation, and unemployment, but there were good grounds for the British to take pride in their productive economy and free institutions.

It was a paradoxical country, both liberal and conservative, both aristocratic and bourgeois, with both a confident landowning governing class and many enterprising and successful businessmen, a country of both acute class consciousness and of upward social mobility, in which both birth and merit could find rewards. It was a wealthy country, but many suffered from poverty. Britons roamed the world, traded and governed in distant places, and accumulated much ethnographic and linguistic knowledge, yet always believed, or so it seemed to irritated outsiders, that their own English ways were the best.

As already explained, the newly installed government of Louis XVIII sent Say on a mission to England to study economic and social conditions in that country. He remained there for four months. He traveled widely, reaching as far north as Glasgow and as far west as Bath and Bristol, and formed friendships that he continued to value in later years, as with Thomas Malthus, James Mill, and Francis Place, and even stayed as a house guest with Jeremy Bentham and David Ricardo. His impressions of England were no doubt formed, and also colored, in conversation with these critics of the established order. He could even sense the influence again of Adam Smith, when at Glasgow he was invited to sit in the chair occupied by Smith as a professor at the University there, and did so with a depth of feeling that he later recalled in his own lectures.

He entitled the published report of his visit of 1814 *De l'Angleterre et des Anglais*. The usual note on translation is in order. The French *Bretagne* means both Britain and Brittany. The French can say *Grande Bretagne*, and more rarely *britannique*, but they really have no convenient word for "British," and so usually say simply *anglais*. In the following pages this word is translated as either "British" or "English" as Say's meaning seems to require—he was well aware of the importance of Scotland.

His report, a pamphlet of fifty-six pages, began as follows:

> The long interruption of communications between France and England has made the short time since the peace very valuable. It has now been possible to cross the Channel to seek an explanation for phenomena of which we know only the results, and to measure the lever that has raised Europe more than once.
>
> It is not the military nor even the naval forces of the British nation that have had so momentous an influence on the continent. Nor will I even say that it is its gold, for since 1797 the British have had only paper money resting on no metallic foundation. Of all the world's nations England is perhaps the one, proportionately speaking, that possesses the least in precious metals. Yet it has wealth and credit, which have been its means of action.
>
> Since these potent weapons arise from its economy, its economic system is its outstanding characteristic and the one that deserves our attention.
>
> Until 1814 France with its ascendancy on the continent and England with the same at sea could not come seriously to grips, and their numerous encounters on one or the other of these elements were no more than skirmishes that could not compromise their existence, nor even their power, however calamitous they were to humanity. But their total effect was to deprive England for almost twenty-three years of its easy and regular contacts with the continent, and France of almost all its overseas connections. Colonies separated from their home countries either became independent or fell prey to the British, into whose hands almost all overseas commerce was gathered. Except for a few adventurous ships, most of which could not escape from the British, it was only

by British vessels, or at least by British permission, that the products of Asia and America could reach our quarter of the globe or the products of European soil and industry be carried to other parts of the world. Whether this preponderance was acknowledged or not, whether trade went on by contraband or by licenses, under fraudulent colors or openly, the fact nevertheless existed.

What were the consequences of this monopoly?

The commercial profits of Great Britain rose to an amazing height. More than 20,000 ships a year entered British ports. New businessmen and new capital came forward to share in the profits. Many new employments of all kinds were created, and since families increase in proportion to their means of earning a living, the population of British maritime cities saw a remarkable growth. London is no longer a city but a province covered with houses. Glasgow, which in 1791 had 66,000 inhabitants, now has 110,000. Liverpool, which in 1801 had a population of 77,000, now has 94,000. Bristol in the same length of time has risen from 63,000 to 76,000.

In a footnote he lists six "manufacturing towns," led by Manchester and Birmingham, showing a similar recent rise in population. He sees what would later be called the industrial revolution, from which, however, the country had yet received no actual benefit.

But while war brought a forced development of British industry the British people profited very little. Taxation and government borrowing took away all the fruits. Taxes, weighing heavily on the products of all classes, removed the clearest portion of their earnings. Government loans absorbed the savings of large entrepreneurs, those most advantageously placed to benefit from changing conditions.

The ease with which the Government could borrow, that is, be able to spend a principal sum so long as it paid the interest, led to enormous outlays. War expenses are greater for England than for any other nation. First of all, the government in obtaining its supplies suffers like other consumers from high prices, of which it is itself the primary cause. Then it pays not only for its own supply but for the supply of its allies, and not only the wages of its own soldiers but those of many other soldiers as well. Its military and naval forces are strewn throughout the globe.

A supply station or storage depot in Asia or America costs twice what it would in Europe. Every soldier sent so far away costs as much as two soldiers, and that is an advantage that the United States will always have in their future troubles with Great Britain.

I say nothing of abuses that are a scandal: old abuses that grow by degrees, new abuses introduced on purpose, abuses exposed by the parliamentary opposition because only friends of the ministers benefit from them, and abuses that the opposition refrains from exposing because the national vanity protects them.

Say's purely rhetorical "I say nothing" is further amplified in a long footnote detailing what "the Nelson family costs the British nation in perpetuity," showing that the widow, brother, and two sisters of Lord Nelson, the deceased admiral and hero of Trafalgar, cost a total of 336,000 francs a year.

> From all this it results that although taxes have quadrupled since 1793 the annual expenditures have progressively exceeded the annual revenues, and that the mounting deficit has been financed by more considerable borrowings from one year to the next, so that finally the principal of the debt has reached the appalling sum of 18 billion, 649 million in French money. When the interest is combined with current consumption we find for the year 1813, for public expenditures of the central government, the incredible sum of 112,391,000 pounds sterling (over 2 billion, 697 million of our money).
>
> On seeing such expense *for only one year*, which has apparently been surpassed for the year 1814, one might think oneself mistaken, but it is founded on official communications and by writers attached to the public service.

His footnotes throughout this passage cite mainly Patrick Colquhoun, *On the Wealth of the British Empire*, Robert Hamilton on the British national debt, and some speeches in parliament. He continues:

> To defray this annual expenditure about 69 million pounds sterling were furnished by taxes for that year. The rest was obtained by loans and anticipations. In other words, about one billion 700 million in our money was raised from the annual income of the British nation and another billion from its capital and savings, and all this without counting taxes for local expenses, the church, and the poor, which are known to add up to considerable sums. It would not be far from the truth to say that the government consumes half of what the soil, capital, and industry of the British people produce.
>
> In moral as in physical science facts are born of each other. One effect becomes the cause of another effect, which in turn becomes a cause. The enormity of the burden on the British people has made all products of their soil and industry exorbitantly expensive. Everything consumed by producers of all classes, and all their movements, so to speak, being taxed, the prices of all output of their industry have risen, without these high prices being of any advantage. . . .

A few paragraphs follow on the bad effects of inflation, a word not yet then used in its economic sense, and whose absence made Say's discussion somewhat desultory and unfocused.

> . . . A businessman in England, if he is not employing his own capital and so must pay interest, cannot support his family. . . .
>
> . . . It is a cause also of distress in the laboring class. . . . It is said that a third of the population of Great Britain must rely on public charity. . . .
>
> When we see such an active, noble, and ingenious nation forced by a bad economic system to make such efforts and yet suffer so many privations, we may ask a bitter question: What good are civil and religious liberty, freedom of the press, security of property, and domination of the seas?
>
> The great misfortune of England is to have had, for many years, successive governments that while making all possible mistakes have never made the mistake of failing in their financial obligations. This regularity [in paying interest] becoming a principle, and joined with the publicity of accounts and the specious edifice of the sinking fund consolidated by Mr. Pitt, has made the credit of the government strong enough to consume the principal value of future income of the British people, to have future generations bear the burden of errors of the present generation, and to multiply tenfold or a hundredfold the importance of these errors by the vast resources that this credit puts in the hands of the political cabinet.

But Say finds that the continuing rise in prices has been in some ways beneficial. It has led to what we would now call greater productivity, or the production of some goods and services at a lower unit cost.

> The need of economizing on all costs of production has nevertheless had some good effects among many bad ones. It has, so to speak, led to improvements in the art of production, with discovery of more expeditious, simple, and hence more economical means of reaching a given objective. Since large enterprises are in general less costly, small ones have become large. I have seen dairies at Glasgow where milk from three hundred cows is sold for two sous. The education of the poor, which may be the only security for the rich, was hindered by the high price of books and wages for teachers, so that within a few years in one of the most civilized nations of Europe there might be no more security than among the Kaffirs. Suddenly someone devised schools in which a single teacher, quickly and successfully, teaches reading, writing, and calculation without books or pens to five hundred children at a time.

Here he has a long footnote explaining what was called the Lancastrian system, in which older or brighter pupils helped to teach the others. He offers it as an example of how private initiative makes up for the folly of government. He then notes the real key to the puzzle of England.

> . . . But it is mainly the introduction of machinery into the arts that has made the production of wealth more economical. There are, for example, now few large farms in England that do not employ threshing-machines, by which on an extensive property more work is done in a day than in a month by the ordinary method.
>
> And finally, human labor, which the high price of consumer's goods has made so expensive, is nowhere replaced so advantageously as by *steam engines*.
>
> They are used in all kinds of work. They move machines for spinning and for the weaving of cotton and wool; they brew beer, and they cut glass. I have seen some that embroider muslin and some that churn butter. At Newcastle and Leeds ambulant steam engines haul wagons full of coal; and nothing is more surprising to the traveler, at first sight, than to meet in the open country these long convoys advancing by themselves without the aid of any living creature.

What Say saw in 1814 were "locomotives," and indeed trains of freight, fifteen years before such things were put on rails from Manchester to Liverpool and so opened the railway age.

> Steam engines have multiplied prodigiously everywhere. There were only two or three in London thirty years ago; now there are thousands. There are hundreds of them in the great manufacturing cities; they are seen even in the country, and industrial work can no longer be kept going advantageously without their powerful support. But they require an abundance of coal, that combustible fossil that nature seems to have put in reserve to supplement the exhaustion of forests, the inevitable result of civilization. With the aid of a simple mineralogical map one could trace an industrial map of Great Britain. There is industry wherever there is coal. . . .
>
> The critical situation of which I have tried to give a picture, and find the causes, is the subject of debates not only in the two houses of Parliament but throughout the whole nation. It gives importance to attacks by the parliamentary opposition, which is less redoubtable for the number of its partisans than by the force of its arguments and the great names and great talents to be found within it.
>
> Grain prices and paper money are the main subjects of these debates. The government has recently legislated on both these matters, but laws are no remedy for difficulties that arise from the nature of things, and problems only reappear with renewed vigor. A few explanations are necessary.

He turns first to the famous Corn Laws, the word "corn" in British usage meaning cereals such as wheat and barley as well as the maize that Americans call corn. British agriculture had been protected for several generations by tariffs and bounties, but in 1815 the protection was heightened, with the import of grain prohibited until the price rose above 80 shillings a quarter. The reader should be reminded also of the meaning of "landowner" and "farmer" in the following passage: the landowners were relatively few, generally of the aristocracy and gentry, each owning many acres, which they leased in large tracts to "farmers," some of them quite well-to-do, who employed hired labor for the actual cultivation.

We saw at the beginning of this survey how circumstances favorable to commerce and manufactures in England also brought on a rising price of grain. But the taxes paid by the cultivator to the state and rentals paid by the farmers to the landowner rose in the same proportion, and now those engaged in agriculture claim that for the price of grain to reimburse the cultivator for his advances it must be maintained at from 95 to 100 shillings a quarter, and hence that importation should be prohibited as soon as the price falls below this level.

They add that unless Parliament adopts this principle it will be impossible for farmers to pay their rentals to the landowners or their taxes to the state, that with the cultivation of grain yielding a loss the less fertile land will be withdrawn from agriculture and the best land turned to other uses, that grain will become more scarce, nothing will be done to avoid rising prices, and the British nation will be more dependent on foreigners for its subsistence.

On the other hand, manufacturers and men in business maintain that if goods of primary necessity remain at such exorbitant prices the cost of labor must rise rather than diminish, with the result that they will offer their products with more disadvantage in foreign markets.

It is a dreadful alternative. Either agriculture and farmers are ruined if grain prices do not rise, or commerce and manufactures are ruined if they do.

Parliament, setting at 80 shillings the price below which grain cannot be imported, has recently found a middle ground that satisfies no one. . . .

The Corn Laws outlived Jean-Baptiste Say. It was not until 1846 that Britain allowed the free importation of grain. The ability of other countries to sell grain to Britain then enabled them to pay for British coal, manufactures and services, and the great era of free trade followed.

Say's treatment of paper money leads him into a discussion of the Bank of England. Founded in 1694 primarily to lend money to the government during its wars against Louis XIV, and receiving government bonds in return, the Bank had soon begun to issue its own bank notes, payable in gold or silver on demand, but in 1797, during the renewed wars with France, it had been authorized by the government to "suspend," that is, discontinue, the conversion of its notes.

The question of banknotes, in theory more thorny [than the Corn Laws], involves less inconvenience in practice. To understand it, one must know the basis of the present monetary system of England, which is rather curious.

The Bank of England is a private company of capitalists which discounts letters of exchange and charges itself, for a fee, with several government services such as the payment of interest on government bonds. It has repeatedly lent to the government not only the sum equal to its stockholders' capital but also sums in banknotes that it issues for this purpose. These notes, consequently, have no security except in government obligations received by the bank in exchange, which pay interest but of which the return of principal cannot be demanded, and which therefore cannot be used for redemption of the very banknotes that these obligations have caused to be issued. . . .

Banknotes loaned to the government, and passed on by the government to its creditors, came back to the Bank for redemption more or less promptly, and especially at times of uncertainty; and the Bank, having received no real exchange values at the time of their issue, was unable to redeem them.

Then either the government had to pay the Bank so that the Bank might redeem its notes, or it had to authorize the Bank not to redeem them. The latter course was adopted in 1797. The suspension of specie payment by the Bank has been renewed several times since then. Its notes have become a veritable paper money, for no one can demand of private persons what private persons cannot demand of the Bank. Debts and commercial paper are no longer paid except in notes, and when anyone buys a bill of exchange payable in England he knows that it will be paid only in banknotes.

Say's further discussion of this subject is too long and complex for intelligible abridgement. He seems to think that paper money might be an acceptable medium if only its value could be stabilized, but that doubts about its future must always interfere with its stabilization. He refers his reader to current writings by Ricardo and his own new *Treatise on Political Economy* of 1814. He concludes by professing himself unable to foresee what will happen to paper money in England.

In fact, only a few years later, in 1821, the Bank of England resumed specie payment. The pound sterling was put on the gold standard and remained there until the First World War. It became, along with the steam engine and railway already mentioned, and free trade after repeal of the Corn Laws, the foundation on which Britain so long enjoyed its superiority as the workshop and financial center of the world.

Say next turns to an account of the East India Company, which he sees as another burden on the British government and people. He returned to the subject in 1824, as will be seen below.

Older than the national debt, the Company had been chartered in 1600 as an association of English merchants with a monopoly for trade east of the Cape of Good Hope, a monopoly justified by the great expense of outfitting, loading, and protecting ships and their cargoes for such long and time-consuming voyages to half-known and potentially dangerous places. For many years the Company engaged in little more than trade, but in the fifty years before Say's tract of 1815 it had also, in the confused situation in India as the Mogul empire disintegrated, become the sovereign authority in large parts of the subcontinent. In the 1770s the British government began to assert its authority, setting up in conjunction with the Company a governor-general and three "governments of India" at Calcutta, Madras, and Bombay, designed more to control British subjects in India than to govern the peoples of India themselves. In 1813 Parliament abolished the Company's monopoly of trade with and within India, leaving it with a monopoly for trade with China. The Company itself lasted until after the Indian Mutiny of 1857. Say begins writing in 1815:

> There is another point not closely related to what I have said, but on which it seems to me that public opinion also needs to be enlightened. It is on the power thought to be derived by England from its colonies, and notably India, a country where a company of British merchants possesses territories larger than the three kingdoms [England, Scotland, and Ireland], and rules over 40 million subjects.
>
> The British can draw wealth from India as sovereigns and as merchants; they can receive tributes and profits.
>
> Let us examine the tributes that they receive as sovereigns.

With figures from Colquhoun's *Wealth of the British Empire* he shows the income of the "governments of India" at about 18 million pounds sterling, but the expenses (for administration, military arrangements, and debt) at 19 million. As a government, the Company operates at an annual loss of about a million. As a commercial concern it earns annual profits of about 700,000.

> These profits, for a company with six millions of capital and 46 millions of debt, are assuredly not very high. Even so, they seem exaggerated. They are an average of four years that are probably better than

others, 1807 through 1810. Several credible writers assert that the stockholders of the Company fail to gain as merchants what they lose as sovereigns, as seems to be confirmed by the loans to which the Company has had to resort for its stockholders not to be deprived of their dividends.

Nevertheless, partisans of the Company claim that it is useful to England even if it operates at a loss.

They say that its expenses in India are mostly for the salaries of its civil and military employees. I agree, but most of these salaries are earned in India; they are also spent there, and add nothing to the power of the British nation in Europe.

They say that the market for British goods in India brings profits to Great Britain. I agree to this also, but if British capital and industry were not applied to India they would be applied to other objectives. What would prevent the British from trading with India, and selling much the same articles, if they were not the dominant power? Sovereignty cannot make people buy what they cannot pay for or what does not suit their customs. If they are offered what suits them they will buy without being subjects.

Here Say has a curious footnote on the island of St. Helena, to which Napoleon was exiled at about the time of his writing, and where he says that the cost of British civilian and military personnel on the island was 84,000 pounds sterling a year, with an income from the island of only 1,200 pounds.

He summarizes with a prophecy of the end of colonialism that proved to be wildly inaccurate in its time scale, in view of the height of European imperialism that came over half a century later, but which by the middle of the twentieth century proved to be correct. In a final conclusion to his *England and the English* he restates his belief in political economy as a means of obtaining at least a partial glimpse of the future.

> . . . In varying degree, it is the same with other British colonies as with India, with this difference, that the government in these other colonies, exercising sovereignty but not engaging in trade, is not compensated by commercial profits for its losses as a sovereign. The old colonial system will fall everywhere in the course of the nineteenth century. There will be no more of the foolish pretension to administer countries that are two, three, or six thousand leagues away. When these countries are independent there will still be a lucrative trade with them, without the cost of all those military and maritime establishments that are like expensive props awkwardly supporting a collapsing building.
>
> Such, from several points of view, is the situation to which events of our time have brought Great Britain. I think I have neither exaggerated

nor disguised the difficulties of its position, for I feel free of precon-
ceived ideas. I wish well for the prosperity of England, as I do for
France and all other countries. Prosperity for one is far from incompat-
ible with prosperity for another, as too many people imagine; it is in fact
favorable. I have tried to set forth some interesting facts and great experiences in political economy, because such experiences are rare and can
be costly. For common minds events only follow one another; for the
thinking man they are connected. Sometimes he may see some of the
links in a chain that joins the present to the future. He will then know
of the future what is permitted to be known, since pythonesses and judicial astrology have gone out of fashion.

Say returned to the subject of the British in India in an article of
1824. By that time he had extended his acquaintance among like-
minded persons in both England and France. In France, he became a
frequent contributor to the *Revue encyclopédique*, a monthly review edited by another old revolutionary and now a liberal of the 1820s, Marc-
Antoine Jullien. All of Say's comments on England in the remainder of
this chapter were published in this French periodical. As for England,
since his visit there in 1814, he had come to know the economists Ricardo and Malthus, the polymath philosopher Jeremy Bentham, and the
economist and historian James Mill. The latter two were leading "utili-
tarians" or Philosophical Radicals. Many of Say's strictures on England
were also expressed by such British writers. Relations could be quite
warm; when James Mill sent his precocious son John Stuart Mill at the
age of fourteen to spend a year in France to improve his education, the
young Mill lived for part of the time as a house guest of the Says in Paris.
What is more important for the present purpose, James Mill produced in
1817, after years of work, a three-volume *History of the British East
India Company*. His book was highly critical of the Company, but he
nevertheless became one of the Company's officials in London in 1819,
and remained so until his death in 1836.

Say's long article of 1824 had a long title: "Essay on the origin and
probable progress of the British sovereignty in India." Its first half told
the earlier history of the Company. We begin with the second half,
where he explains how the territorial conquests by the Company had
been financed by loans from the British government and so had been
enormously costly to "the government, or rather the nation."

> All these embarrassments, as well as other causes that need not be
> gone into, have gradually brought the Company into complete depen-
> dence on the British ministry. Its directors, sitting in London, have the
> appearance of administering the domains of the Company through its
> agents, since these agents are its paid employees. But in 1784 the minis-

try was authorized by Parliament to form a permanent council called the Board of Control, which is normally composed of the principal minister and his creatures. The directors are obliged to obtain the agreement of this Board for appointments to vacancies and all political and military operations. It is the Board that really governs. The directors enjoy a certain independence only in their commercial activities.

Appointment to vacant posts in both Europe and Asia, or confirmation of their official powers, adds considerably to the means of influence and corruption in the hands of the crown.

It is estimated that the Company at present employs 15,000 civilian agents in India, of whom 3,000 are Europeans; 160,000 soldiers and officers, of whom 20,000 are Europeans, and notably all the officers; and 25,000 sailors; which brings the number of its paid employees to 200,000.

After further particulars on the huge expenses, loans, and debts recently incurred for conquests in India by the Marquess of Wellesley (brother of the Duke of Wellington) during the Napoleonic Wars in Europe, Say goes on:

> All this information is drawn from Adam Smith, from Colquhoun, from the estimable works of Robert Hamilton on the public debt, and above all from the excellent *History of British India* published in 1817 by Mr. James Mill.
>
> A reader of Mill's book will hardly be surprised to learn that the East India Company is so prodigiously in debt, both in India and in Europe, especially since, despite its losses, it has never ceased to pay its stockholders a dividend of 10 percent. In 1805 it acknowledged a debt of 150 millions in England, and of 640 millions in India, for a total of 790 millions. But I note that it reaches this figure only after allowing for deductions to which it believes itself entitled. If these deductions are for the most part unlikely or impossible to be realized, they should not be counted as an asset useful for diminishing the debt.

These deductions were, he claims, made by the company for reduction of its debt to the government, in consideration of expense for maintaining military forces in India, an expense which the government thought it had incurred for the benefit of the Company, and was unwilling to assume. After thus finding that the Company understates its liabilities, Say proceeds to show how it overstates its assets.

> What are we to think, for example, of the value of its forts, warehouses, and other buildings with their furnishings, which it counts among its assets? These things cannot have a value for anyone else equal to their cost to the Company on which the valuation is based. Nor are

they a disposable value for a government, as they would be for a private person. When a private person makes improvements worth 50,000 *écus* on land worth 100,000, he can reasonably expect, because of the capital he has expended, to sell such a property for 150,000 *écus*. The improvements are alienable, because the land is. But a government only enjoys the usufruct of its possessions. When these pass to a succeeding government, the new government owes nothing to the old for the public establishments transferred to it. Such establishments are thought to have been made for public utility; by the services they render to the public they continue to pay a kind of interest on the cost of their creation. . . .

Other receivables claimed by the India Company are no more capable of realization. For example, the Company lists as an asset 43 millions for an expedition that it sent to Egypt when Bonaparte occupied that country. But this expense was incurred by the Company more in its own interest than in that of the British government, which does not recognize this debt. The British government would have better grounds for asking the government of India to reimburse it for the costs of Nelson's fleet and the expedition that took Egypt from the French. At the very least, the two counterclaims annul each other.

Or again, a sum of 50 millions is indicated as due to the Company from the nabob of Arcot and the rajah of Tanjore, but these two princes are not likely to pay this debt to a Company that since then has conquered their territory and left them without resources.

Since these dubious assets amount to at least 400 millions, and cannot be deducted as the Company claims from its acknowledged debt of 790 millions, they leave the principal of its debt at nearly 1,200 millions of our money.

The British East India Company can thus be seen as both a commercial and a sovereign operation that gains nothing from either its sovereignty or its commerce, and is reduced to borrowing every year the funds to provide its shareholders with a semblance of profit.

He gives reasons to believe, as he had done in 1815, that the British could trade as profitably with India without the Company as with it. In any case, the true source of wealth for any country is not to be sought outside its own borders:

. . . To find the source of a people's wealth we must not look for it in foreign countries; it must be sought in the bosom of the people itself. The wise and active industry of the British, the order and economy seen in their heads of enterprises, the protection they find in equal laws for all—these are the mines from which they extract their treasures, and these mines are within the reach of all nations.

What then will become of the British sovereignty in India? It would be a rash man who thought himself able to give a positive answer to such a question. No one can pierce the mysteries of the future, but it is possible to see some events as more probable, some as less probable, and some as impossible. At each renewal of its privilege the Company and the British government, from a confused feeling of their own position and interests, have gradually tended toward a liberation of trade and a replacement of the sovereignty of the Company by the sovereignty of the State. The last renewal of the privilege, made in 1813 to last until 1834, provides that any subject of the British empire may trade freely with India on obtaining permission from the directors of the Company; but this permission cannot be refused, for if its directors raise an obstacle the Board of Control will decide. The exclusive privilege of the Company now applies only to trade with China.

It is hence clear that the Company hardly depends on trade with India properly so called, and that its sovereignty has escaped it. It depends more for its profits on trade with China, because tea and certain grades of silk and nankeen can only be obtained there, so that British customers must go through the Company. But soon the British will be its only customers for merchandise brought from Canton. Other navigators, especially the Americans, will supply other nations more cheaply. The British themselves will grow tired of paying exaggerated costs of production, and to raise its tariff revenues the government will probably do away with this last refuge of the monopoly. I should not be surprised if the present privilege is not renewed at its expiration in 1834, or to see India governed by a viceroy and the Company's debt made part of the national debt.

Then the Company would continue to trade in competition with all British subjects as simply a commercial concern, and would probably be gradually liquidated, as unable to sustain the competition of a free commerce. If these events do not come sooner it will be because of private interests, which in this case, as always, prolong the duration of abuses.

Say's predictions came true, but only after suppression of the Indian Mutiny of 1857, when the East India Company was finally dissolved, its debt merged into the national debt, and the head of the British government in India was raised to the rank of Viceroy.

He next examines the possible political future of India, which he does not find encouraging. If, he says, the hard-working and ingenious people of India should become independent they would still not understand what is needed for self-government; if the British in India should become independent from England they would be hopelessly outnumbered in India; if some outside power, European or other, should attempt a conquest it would become embroiled in civil wars among Indian princes. But if the political situation is unpromising, there is hope that India may share in the progress of civilization.

In any case, the liberation of India seems impossible. But in the interest of the human race should we desire that the European nations should lose their influence in Asia? Should we not wish, on the contrary, that this influence should grow? Europe is not what it was in the time of Vasco da Gama and Albuquerque. It has reached the point where Asia should no longer fear its domination. With its despots and superstitions Asia has no good institutions to lose, and can receive many good ones from Europeans.

These latter, because of their distinctive genius for enterprise and the astonishing progress they have made in all branches of human knowledge, are doubtless destined to subdue the world as they have already subdued the two Americas. I do not say that they will subdue it by force of arms; military predominance is and will increasingly be contingent and precarious. The Europeans will subdue the world by the inevitable ascendancy of enlightenment and institutions that operate without respite. Europeans no longer need to use armed force against the indigenous peoples of America. Asia will take more time because of its immense population and the inertia of tenacious and immovable ways of life opposed to all kinds of innovation.

But the force of things carries all before it. The religion of the Magi yielded to Islam; the religion of Brahma has lost half the territory where it once reigned; Islam will wear away in its turn, as everything does. Seaborne communications are constantly improved. In our time voyages from the Cape of Good Hope to Bengal are twice as easy and more rapid than they were before 1789. Other routes to the Orient will undoubtedly become more practicable and shorter. The liberation of Greece will bring that of Egypt. Civilization as it spreads will smooth out the obstacles to communication, for the more the peoples of the world become civilized the more they perceive their interest in communicating with one another. Then we shall see what the world will be one day; but time is a necessary element in all great revolutions.

It is with this declaration of faith in the progress of civilization that Say's survey of the British in India concludes. It has so far proved to be a less accurate prophecy than some of his others.

He was more severely critical of the British in Ireland than in India, as he showed in an article in the *Revue encyclopédique* for November 1828. Ireland had been a possession of the English crown since the twelfth century, when the Norman conquest of England was followed by an

Anglo-Norman invasion of the smaller island. As a separate kingdom from England, though ruled by the same king, it enjoyed several troubled centuries of Anglo-Irish Catholic supremacy until the time of Henry VIII, who after transforming the English Catholic church into an Anglican communion introduced a similar arrangement in Ireland, where a legally established Church of Ireland took over the properties, tithes, parishes, and bishoprics of its Catholic predecessor, while the mass of the population remained Roman Catholic. Irish rebellions followed, always put down, with massacres on both sides; landed estates were confiscated and handed over to English owners; and in the seventeenth century, in the "plantation of Ulster," a population of Protestant farmers and workers, mostly Scottish, was settled in the northern part of the island. During the English revolution of 1689 Ireland again played a part; the deposed James II attempted to regain his throne with the aid of Irish Catholic sympathizers and 7,000 French infantry who had landed in Ireland, but he was defeated by William III at the battle of the Boyne near Dublin. With the recurrent Anglo-French wars of the following century, Ireland remained a source of strategic concern for the British.

In the 1790s the United Irish attempted a revolution, expecting aid from France in the hope of setting up an independent Irish republic on the French model. This too was suppressed; Ireland lost its separate parliament and was incorporated into the United Kingdom. The Irish could now send representatives to the combined parliament at Westminster, but only on the terms applying to the "unreformed" House of Commons, in which, as noted, until 1829 Roman Catholics were unable to sit.

Thus the perennial Irish question in 1828 was at one of its climactic moments, the issue being whether Roman Catholics should be allowed to sit in the House of Commons. In fact, only a few months later, in April 1829, the act of Catholic Emancipation became law against strong opposition, making Irish (and English) Catholics eligible for election to the House. But Say's article was not thereby outdated, for it treated other Irish grievances that were only slowly relieved.

Say, with his good knowledge of English, seized upon a word then new, "absenteeism," referring to absentee landlords. He called his article "Absenteeism: Or What will Become of Ireland?" He began:

> A British admiral, a member of the House of Commons, has had the misfortune of saying openly in parliament that it would be a good thing for England if Ireland could be swallowed up by the sea for twenty-four hours; and what is still worse, he told the truth, thanks to the bad institutions that prevail in that unhappy country. They have in fact produced for England an ulcer, or cancer, that eats at it and will end by

killing it. Thoughtful people in England know this, and are beginning to be disturbed. Ireland was subjugated by force, and there has never been any amalgamation. The larger island has devoured the smaller but been unable to digest it. There is only one British Isle; the other remains the Isle of Erin, or Ireland.

It will be asked why such vicious institutions are not corrected. It is a natural question; but it is like asking, Why not cure cancer? It carries its malignancy within itself. The Irish peasant is Catholic, and his prejudices make it his duty to support the priests of his religion; but the Anglican priests will not give up their tithes, which they collect with rigor. How to persuade them that everyone should pay for his own religion? Aren't the lords spiritual in the upper house there to protect them? Don't they also have their tithes to defend?

The Irish rebelled before submitting; what followed was natural, there were massacres and land confiscations, it was all very simple. But in other countries revolution is a passing cloudburst. Properties after changing hands are well cared for by their new owners, often better than by the old, and the country prospers more than ever. In Ireland, on the contrary, landed property was not sold but given out to supporters of the new dynasty, the ancestors of the Castlereaghs, Wellingtons, Beresfords, and many others. These people, unable to live agreeably or even safely in a country thus treated, returned to England after leasing their lands to speculators who sublet them in small lots to poor peasants who outbid each other to obtain a portion, and who thought themselves fortunate if after paying their rent they had enough potatoes left to avoid starvation.

Such is the regime for which a new word has been found, *absenteeism*, which some defend without blushing.

It is understandable that those who gorge themselves in England on the sweat of the Irish people, and who occupy the higher offices of government, cannot consent in good faith to renunciation of abuses from which they profit; but that writers who ought to be independent, and philosophers who profess love of the public good, should lend support to such a pernicious order of things; that they should insult political economy by claiming that such an abominable abuse of force is founded on its principles, is something not to be tolerated. In general, a man who consumes his whole income does not alter the national capital; but when he consumes his income in a foreign country (and nothing is more foreign to Ireland than England), his consumption does nothing to favor continuing production. The manner of consumption is not indifferent; some portion of the income of the rich is always productively reinvested, as in improvement of the soil, or of buildings or means of communication. If all such elements of prosperity are spread upon English ground by means of income drawn from Ireland, it is hard to persuade us that no harm is done to the latter country.

Abstract principles will make no one accept what revolts common sense. An engineer after building a bridge that falls down will never prove to me by his algebra that it should have stood up. Nor will Mr. McCulloch prove to me that the despoilers of Ireland are not to be blamed for consuming, at a great distance, the product of a war indemnity that they oblige the Irish people to pay to them every year. The only sound political economy is not a science of abstractions; it is a practical and experimental science like physics and chemistry. Its glory is to explain facts, not to contradict them. It is thus that Adam Smith conceived of it, and it is why his book has enjoyed lasting success and been translated into all languages. But for that, it must express only what is both useful and true.

To return to Ireland, and to the evils it suffers from *absenteeism*: After recognizing that the condition of that island is violent and contrary to nature, we may ask how it all should end, for I do not suppose any general rallying to the philanthropic wish for its total submersion. What would be desirable would be for the lands given out to reward the defenders of religion and ruling dynasties to be restored to their former owners, or sold for the benefit of Ireland; for the church establishment to be suppressed, and the Irish allowed to profess whatever religion they prefer, while paying for their own priests. Then what would happen would be like what has happened in Scotland, where the Presbyterian majority has no tithes to pay, acquits only its part in the general revenues of the State, and shares in the employments and the protection that the State owes to its citizens. Gradually Ireland would identify itself with England and become a valuable province of the British empire. But the enemies of the British empire, if there are any, may rest assured. Even if the English could rid themselves of the national egoism with which they are reproached, their profound contempt for what is different from themselves, it is not possible for the powerful interests opposing such a desirable reform to be overcome. There could be no complete revolution, for the English populace itself would revolt at the idea of calling Irishmen their brothers.

The evil will therefore continue, and its progress will be rapid.

At this point Say introduces a long quotation from a then recent book by an English physician who had spent several years in Ireland, and who predicts that hordes of penniless Irish will soon pour into England, since steamships have now made the passage of the Irish Sea so rapid and easy, and that their competition for jobs will drive down the living standards of English workers. Say goes on:

. . . The English believe that the population of Ireland will always exceed the means of subsistence, and that no concessions can prevent its
people from overflowing into England. I, too, think that the human
race is the same everywhere, and that population will always press upon
the means of subsistence; but this is not the present case, for Ireland
exports great quantities of foodstuffs, wheat, and salted meat which its
producers never touch. It is well known that ships bound for America
almost all stop at Cork or Waterford to complete their stores of provisions. The island also contains much uncultivated land and wetlands
that can be drained; its agriculture under a better regime could be
much more highly developed. What is lacking in Ireland is not subsistence but the ability to pay for it. With landowners far away, without
capitalists who might introduce productive businesses, and with numerous government employees, ecclesiastics, and military personnel to
feed, heavy taxes to pay, and the ignorance resulting from so many evils,
the Irish simply lack the means of improving their condition. They have
only one consolation, and they use it; the population keeps growing,
and so does poverty. With a less harsh existence they would think more
of the future; they would accumulate a bit more savings and fewer children; they would become more civilized; but it is not for the English to
provide them with any such less harsh existence—as all peoples who
have been subjected by the English might agree.

The streaming of destitute Irish into northern England and southern
Scotland, exacerbating the problems of low wages and unemployment
that already afflicted those areas, called Say's attention to a report published by the British parliament, which he reviewed in the *Revue encyclopédique*. It was the report of a special committee of the House of
Commons on emigration and colonization. It recommended a policy of
financially assisted emigration, which in fact went into effect. During the
fifty years ending in 1878, when the policy was discontinued, about
350,000 emigrants were officially assisted. It was a small proportion of
the 8,500,000 who are estimated to have left Great Britain and Ireland
in those years, most of whom went to the United States and many to
Canada and Australia. But assisted emigration was important in establishing the first British settlements in South Africa and New Zealand.

Say's article is of interest both for the facts that it presents and for the
admiration he expresses for public parliamentary inquiries as conducted
in England. (He had been more scornful of the one that questioned
Benjamin Franklin in 1766.) He now wrote:

This overflow of Irish workers is a menace to both England and Scotland. Manchester is infected. It will be necessary to use armed force to
drive away these unfortunate inhabitants of another province of the

same country; otherwise, the whole working class of Scotland and England, that is, of the richest and most industrious countries of Europe, would have to sleep in shanties, drink water, and eat potatoes as their only food.

This is the situation faced by the parliament of the British empire. There is a proposal to adopt a general measure on colonization, so that able-bodied but unemployed families can be transported to the numerous British colonies that have great tracts of land yet to be developed. If many indigent families could take this course, the home country would be relieved of many of the poor that it is obliged to assist, and those who remained, being fewer, would not be without work. The difficulty is to provide the cost of their passage and their maintenance overseas until such time as they could live on income from their own products. . . . Such is the object of legislative measures now proposed, which have been assigned to a special committee. To proceed with the mature consideration that they bring in England to such a matter, and which ought to exist everywhere, the committee conducted hearings from February to June 1827.

It is known that a parliamentary committee, on payment of a suitable indemnity, has the right to summon any person whose testimony may serve to enlighten it. It calls by preference on persons who have local knowledge and a reputation for judgment and probity. The witness replies to numerous questions put to him; and the questions and answers are printed in an official record that becomes a repository of facts and opinions to substantiate the final report and enlighten public discussion.

In this present inquiry, where the question is to ascertain the extent and kind of distress from which workers in a certain district suffer, those summoned as witnesses include workers themselves, leading manufacturers, parish vestrymen charged with distribution of poor relief, members of friendly societies, even the bishop of the diocese, and in short anyone believed to be in a position to know the true state of affairs.

When the question is to learn the conditions in the undeveloped regions of Canada, the kinds of agriculture for which they are suited, the facilities available for the necessities of life and for marketing the new settlers' products, the persons consulted are those who have long lived in the colony and seen many new settlements formed, such as merchants who have provided tools and textiles to the settlers and received payment for their products, and civil and military engineers who have mapped the region, determined boundaries, etc. The same questions are put to persons with a knowledge of the Cape of Good Hope, or New South Wales, or Van Diemen's Land [Tasmania]; and the result is such a mass of information that an unenlightened policy cannot be carelessly adopted.

The evils calling for remedies are thus understood, and estimates are possible of the difficulties they present and the means that exist for overcoming them. Remarkable good sense is shown in the answers of witnesses to the questions addressed to them. There is no wandering from the subject; the replies are to the point; no one tries to shine or simply to press for his own opinion. The witnesses all say *I think* or *I don't know*. It is true that members of the committee, and notably its chairman Mr. Wilmot Horton, have a good understanding of the *economy of societies*, more commonly known as *political economy*.

He continues by quoting, verbatim and at length, the exchange of questions and answers with several witnesses, including one who had just returned from eight years in Upper Canada [Ontario], and even the economist Thomas Malthus, who in effect testified that he thought the situation in Ireland to be hopeless. The ensuing potato famine of the 1840s and mass emigration from Ireland seemed to confirm this sad prophecy.

There was more that Say could wholeheartedly endorse in the new University *at* London, as he at first called it, founded in 1828. What he described was actually University College, London, with closing remarks on King's College founded at the same time by members of the Church of England. The very word "university" was of uncertain meaning. There were as yet no real universities in the United States; at Oxford and Cambridge the real entities were the colleges; the universities of Scotland and the Continent combined secondary studies with higher faculties of law, medicine, and theology; the "university of France" as designed by Napoleon consisted primarily of several hundred secondary schools. In many countries, however, more specialized technical institutions had grown up since the eighteenth century, such as the *grandes écoles* in France of which the Polytechnique was the most famous, and the Conservatory of Arts and Trades of which much has been said, and will be said, in this book. As for the University of London, it was later incorporated as a kind of holding company or examining and degree-awarding body for University College, King's College, and after 1900 many others such as the London School of Economics.

Say admired the new institution as a private enterprise, founded by the private initiative of prominent Dissenters, that is, non-Anglicans, and so unaffiliated with the government or any officially favored religion. It will be seen, however, that he approved of its powers to enforce strict moral conduct.

The foundation of the University of London is an event in the progress of the human mind. London is now the largest city in Europe, and perhaps the world. A population of 1,200,000 inhabitants, more wealth than has been brought together anywhere on the globe in the same area, an assemblage of men of merit worthy to be fellow citizens of the Bacons, Newtons, and Lockes, all such circumstances have long seemed to call for a grand center of public instruction that did not exist. If anything should be surprising, it is not that a University should be created at London now, but that it was not created sooner.

Philosophy and enlightenment have benefited from the delay. Other universities were founded by the ascendant political or sacerdotal powers, and they show only too clearly the effects of their origin. Their function was to recruit the priestly caste; or the political authority wished to guide studies in its own interest, to keep out ideas that might elevate man in his own eyes, or to have nurseries of flatterers or efficient servants. Even the most recently formed of these institutions, the one that Napoleon hoped to make a title to his glory, had as its main object the shaping of future generations according to his personal views. The government meddled in everything, directed everything, hardly recognized the rights of parental authority, and subjected genius itself to its own narrow compass.

The University now forming at London is more of our own time. It is the work of the English nation, not of a dynasty or a religious body. All who by their talents, fortune, or social position can take part in this noble project are welcome. The old universities of Oxford and Cambridge are inadequate in many ways. Oxford gives instruction only to those professing the Anglican religion; oaths are required that are sometimes offensive to conscience or common sense. Although Cambridge has relaxed some of its ancient regulations and admits students from dissident sects, it does not allow them to take degrees. Expenses at both universities are excessive, and families for which they are a burden, if they wish their sons to be admitted, must register their names several years in advance.

It may be added that law and medicine are not taught at these universities, and that their degrees are conferred at so late an age that young men cannot most usefully prepare for lucrative professions, or enter at the beginning levels into important social functions.

It has not been possible to find a satisfactory answer to these objections. Hence the University of Edinburgh, or the universities of Germany and the higher schools in France have been preferred to pedantic institutions that had some usefulness in former times, but which the progress of our age, and of enlightenment, has left behind.

London has been chosen as the seat of this new university because of its own importance and its relations with all British possessions. The founders calculate that the capital alone has five thousand young men from sixteen to twenty-one years old whose families are able to support the necessary costs. But a preponderant reason is the ease in obtaining professors in a great capital, the ordinary meeting-place of many men with abilities in all fields of interest.

The site chosen is between Upper Gower Street and the New Road, the cleanest and best aired part of London, and as accessible from all quarters as is possible in so vast a city. It is an area of about seven acres. The structure, of which the parts to be first used have already been built, is composed of a main building 430 feet long, with two large wings that will together form three sides of a quadrangle. . . .

He goes on to tell of lecture halls designed for 440 students, other class-rooms only a little less large, laboratories, offices for the professors, a ceremonial hall, and a museum and library with their exact dimensions.

For intervals between classes the students will have the use of courts, gardens, and lounges, as well as a dining hall, and in the library and museums they can make good use of their moments of leisure. But there are no lodgings for students, or even for professors, in the buildings.

The founders are composed of donors in the strict sense and of stock-holders or proprietors on the model of corporations. The university will be a favored object for testamentary bequests. It will receive certain fees from the students, from which will come most of the honoraria of the professors, who will thus have a direct interest in making their teaching attractive and useful. It seems certain that these forms of income will be sufficient not only to pay a four percent interest to the stockholders but also for a continuing enlargement of the libraries and collections. Two lists of donors and subscribers have been published, already showing nine hundred names of the most highly respected persons in England. . . .

He gives the names of twenty-four members of the governing council of the university. It includes reformers and liberals of various social stations: four members of the House of Lords and five of the House of Commons; James Mill, Joseph Hume, and George Birkbeck; and two young activists and future famous historians, George Grote and T. B. Macaulay. Indeed, his idea of reforming the universities through a market economy, and making their professors depend on the incentive of student fees for their incomes, goes back to Adam Smith.

So we have an immense establishment for public instruction, absolutely free under the surveillance of law, but in which government cannot interfere with a view to producing monks or courtiers as it might wish. The founders will enjoy certain privileges, as in the admission of students. The university will have no police power beyond its own premises. But it will offer some guarantees to families and teachers by recognizing private tutors and operators of student lodging houses

only so far as they are worthy of confidence. The university has announced what it requires of these proprietors of student lodgings: that
they enforce regular moral habits, allow none of their boarders to return at night at unduly late hours or lead a dissipated life, and even require attendance at the public observance of some religion or other, as
seems necessary to preserve tolerance for all. They must report
promptly to the university administration any irregularity in conduct or
health, and accept no one as a boarder unless he is a student. They will
be approved by the University only if they fulfill these conditions,
which are clearly in the interest of young men and their families. We
should not be surprised if, given these conditions, students come to the
University of London from all parts of the civilized world. Although
the University of Edinburgh is much farther from the center of Europe,
we know that Europe is full of medical doctors, professors, and learned
men who are kept away from Oxford and Cambridge by their intoler-
ance and expense, and who testify to the solidity of studies to be found
at Edinburgh.

The first stone of the new edifice was laid on April 30, 1827. . . .
Since that time construction has gone on with a speed that does honor
to the English nation and the enterprise of private persons. Students are
registering in very large numbers. They are given the opportunity to
talk with the professors. The professors question them on the level of
instruction that they have reached, and prepare their lectures accord-
ingly. Classes will begin next October. The whole course of study will
take four years, but the student, if sufficiently advanced, may begin at
the second or even a later year. . . .

About a dozen professors had already been appointed and made public
announcement of what they proposed to teach. Say summarizes and
comments on the list, which in its comprehensive scope could be rivaled
by few if any universities at that time. The subjects included Greek,
Latin, Hebrew, and mathematics, as could be found elsewhere, but also
physics, astronomy, chemistry, "industrial arts," botany, zoology, law,
legislation, political economy, and modern languages. The chairs in history and moral philosophy had not yet been filled. Say's account of political economy and modern languages is of interest in the present context. The professor of political economy was to be John McCulloch, on
whom Say's judgment was now more favorable than what he had said of
McCulloch in connection with Ireland.

This new science of political economy will be professed by Mr. Mc-
Culloch, who has given proofs of his thinking in several courses of public lectures in London, and in several excellent articles in the *Encyclope-
dia Britannica* and the *Edinburgh Review*, a journal put out by the

leading writers of Great Britain, which is irreproachable except for being too exclusively of the Whig party, and for containing ridiculous diatribes against the French character and the learned men of our nation.

Mr. McCulloch says that he will set forth the circumstances most favorable to the greatest production of wealth (that is, of products useful to human needs and desires) with the least possible labor. According to him, all improvements obtained or to be expected in the great art of procuring things indispensable, useful, or agreeable to human life can be classified under one of three headings: (1) the security of properties, (2) the accumulation of capital, and (3) the introduction of exchanges. Several other important subjects are closely related to these three, such as money, contracts, and population.

The professor, after treating the production of wealth, will explain its distribution, for every individual who does not live by the free munificence of someone else subsists by what he can himself draw from his land, his capital, or his labor, so that it is important to know how these portions of income come about. . . .

In the second part of his course the professor will examine the effects of various plans adopted or proposed for assistance to the needy. He will then explore the laws that affect the consumption of wealth; that is, he will distinguish between productive and unproductive consumption. This, it may be noted, is the plan followed by an economist of another nation [obviously Say himself], who like Mr. McCulloch is a disciple of Adam Smith and has sought to complete the doctrine of that famous Scotsman.

We cannot too much applaud this learned professor when he promises to teach his audience to judge for themselves, to examine all questions candidly, describe rather than dogmatize, be slow in their conclusions, and trust only in the results of careful and laborious investigations. . . .

Clearly the founding of London University was part of the general movement for reform then gathering strength in England. Neither here nor elsewhere does Say comment on reform of elections to the House of Commons, to be soon accomplished by the reform bill of 1832. But, as he says, the professor of political economy is to discuss poor relief, soon to be transformed by the memorable New Poor Law of 1834. And Say also notes that the two professors of "legislation" and of "positive law" will go beyond the mysteries and chicaneries of the English common law. They will escape from the "ruts of English jurisprudence" with its "national prejudices" and insist on the need of "more broadly expanded views."

He next turns to the modern languages, which had never been taught anywhere at a university level. There will be professors of German, Italian, and Spanish at the University of London, though none in French had yet been provided for. Say's few ideas on this subject were purely conventional, except for some curious remarks on the future of English. He speculated on the future of the English language in America, as various Americans such as Noah Webster were then doing.

> The living languages and modern literatures will occupy an important place at the University of London, and will be one of the traits that most fully distinguish it from all existing universities.
>
> The English language and literature will have Mr. Thomas Sale for a professor. His course will naturally have two parts, grammar and composition. The latter will deal with precepts and examples; that is, it will be an examination of the rules known to be most useful in composition, with criticism of writers who have made a mark in various kinds of composition in both poetry and prose.
>
> A difficulty presents itself in the study of the English language and literature, a difficulty that only the future can resolve. It is of the essence of living languages to be progressive. New words and new expressions come in with new tastes and needs. In this matter a great nation imposes its laws on all populations that speak its language; but when there are two great nations that have the same idiom, are located in two different hemispheres, and have different and possibly even opposed governments, interests, and opinions, can they go on constantly speaking the same language? If they are to differ in this element of civilization, which of the two will make law for the other? Great Britain and the United States still speak the same language, but will they always do so? And when differences become manifest, which of the two systems is to be followed? Each will preach for its own way; when they communicate will they understand one another? And as for persons who are foreign to both, will they have to undertake two lines of study instead of one? Something nearly analogous seems to have happened between Spanish and Portuguese. There may be a similarity between what has happened to the idioms of the Iberian Peninsula and what will happen in the New World.

Say here obviously anticipates a real problem, but without the necessary distinctions and qualifications. He did not see, for example, that phonetic, colloquial, regional, dialectical, and class variations existed within both Great Britain and the United States as well as between them, and that nevertheless a standard language would remain virtually identical in grammar and vocabulary for all speakers of English.

Say concluded his account of London University with a few words on what became King's College. He had a low opinion of it, and was less than fair; his only purpose was to show by contrast the superiority of the new "university," that is, the University College that he had described at length.

> The Tory party, which counts all the bishops in its ranks and is now protected by the Duke of Wellington as prime minister, is working as much as it can against establishment of the University of London and the propagation of enlightenment. For this purpose it uses tactics learned from the Jesuits of France. It is founding in London, alongside the University, another school in which only the old ideas will be taught by the old methods. This is fortunate, for it will provide evidence of the results in both cases. Coming from one of these schools we shall see fanatics and upholders of all the old prejudices and abuses of which the English nation is growing weary. The other will produce men of merit, who are up to the level of their time and are animated by the enlightened patriotism on which the prosperity of a country rests. It is true that a bad administration does not put men into office by merit, but a bad administration of affairs does not last forever.

It is clear from what has been said that Say's interest in England, first fully expressed in the report of his visit in 1814 and later in articles published in the *Revue encyclopédique*, continued through the rest of his life. His judgments on postwar conditions in Great Britain, the Bank of England, the East India Company, Ireland, and the new London University were all applications of his ideas in economics. We have encroached on the theme of the next chapter, in which we consider some other occasional writings by the first professor of political economy in France.

Chapter 6

THE PROFESSOR OF POLITICAL ECONOMY

THERE WERE SOME in the government of the Bourbon Restoration who wished to promote the economic development of France, and for this purpose took steps to revitalize the Conservatory of Arts and Trades. This establishment, initiated during the Revolution, had languished since that time, remaining a place where workers and their employers could learn about new techniques and inventions. J.-B. Say had praised it in 1798 and had made use of its facilities in 1804 to prepare himself as owner and manager of a cotton spinning plant. The innovators after 1815 proposed to expand the work of the Conservatory by adding three lecture courses—two in the applied sciences of chemistry and mechanics, and one in the applied social science of political economy.

For a chair in this subject J.-B. Say was the obvious and best-known candidate. He was already giving public lectures at a private institution, the Athénée, which was private in the sense of not being financed or sponsored by the state, and public in that any interested person could attend upon payment of a fee. In connection with these lectures he published his short "catechism" on political economy. Every two or three years he brought out a new edition of his *Treatise*, which was known internationally. In 1818 he delivered an address at Malaga, Spain, to inaugurate a chair in political economy in that city. When Ricardo's *Principles of Political Economy and Taxation* appeared in English in 1817 a French translation soon followed, accompanied by extensive notes by Say, provided at the request of the French publisher. Hardly had Malthus published his *Principles of Political Economy* in 1820 when he received a series of long letters from Say, published in both English and French in the same year of 1820, in which Say criticized Malthus's views on various economic questions.

Some in the government, however, were made uneasy, as Napoleon had been, by the very words "political economy." The word "political" seemed to imply that persons outside the government, claiming superior knowledge, might try to tell the government what to do, or object publicly to its policies, or enter into such party politics as now existed. A compromise was reached by which the subject to be taught at the Conservatory would be called "industrial economy." Say was appointed in 1820 to a chair so designated. Strictly speaking, he became a professor of political economy only in 1831, when appointed to a new chair under that title at the College of France, soon after the revolution of 1830, and unfortunately soon before his own death. In any case the name was of secondary importance. Say himself once observed that "political economy" was a misnomer, and that the subject might better have been called "social economy," since its findings affected society as a whole and not merely political matters.

Those interested in upgrading the Conservatory turned for advice to the Academy of Sciences. A committee was formed, of which one member and perhaps its chairman was L. J. Thénard, a distinguished chemist and member of the Academy, who in turn sought advice from J.-B. Say. The amicable relationship between the natural and social sciences is to be noted. We have Say's reply to Thénard, dated 1818, as found among his unpublished papers by his editors of 1848. In the letter, as in Say's inaugural lecture to the chair two years later, we can see that he willingly adopted the phrase *économie industrielle*, and even seemed to use "political" and "industrial" economy interchangeably. Where elsewhere he held that economics should be made understandable to a wide audience, he would have the professorship designed for *entrepreneurs d'industrie*. In these contexts it may be recalled that an *industrie* might be any field of productive activity, and an *art* any practical application of knowledge; and indeed an *entrepreneur*, if the anachronism could be tolerated, might be called a businessman. Say's course in the 1820s anticipated not only later professorships of economics but also the business schools of the twentieth century.

Here is the letter to Thénard of 1818:

> You have asked me, Monsieur, to give you some ideas on how the teaching of Political Economy in a special school of industry may be useful. . . . Please note that I write on the supposition that the course in question is intended for *entrepreneurs in manufactures*, or the heads of such enterprises rather than *ordinary workers*. The latter need only the instruction to be received in shops, and can most successfully learn only there. But the heads need other kinds of knowledge than can be found in shops, and the spread of these kinds is what makes a higher school of industry truly useful.
>
> The arts do not produce a country's wealth simply by the processes that they employ. Those processes may be admirable in their invention and execution, as with some masterpieces of the woodturner's art, which may arouse a sterile admiration but add nothing to the fortune of their creators or to the public wealth, which is only the total wealth of individual persons. We have collections full of ingenious ideas that have had no results, or only bad results; and we see every day people with imagination, or even some well versed in chemistry and mechanics, who fail in all their undertakings.

There is then something to be learned other than the best processes in the arts. It is to know *how and in what way the arts contribute to the formation of values*, which are the true constituents of wealth. The entrepreneur in any kind of commerce or manufacturing should be instructed on this point, because he is the one who combines the efforts with the results, the means with the ends, the advances with the products. If some such men are successful without instruction it is because they routinely follow the right direction, but it is always safer to know why this direction is the right one. This is what Political Economy teaches; I mean political economy of the new school, *Experimental political economy.*

We note here that since the French *expérience* and *expérimental* both refer to what English knows as "experience" and "experiment," Say means that political economy deals with life as lived and the world as observed, that is, experience. He made it clear later, in his inaugural lecture to the chair at the Conservatory, that economists could not provide experiments as in a laboratory.

The systematic part of a science is in the consequences drawn from facts; the essential part is in the knowledge of the facts themselves, i.e., the way in which things happen. We may reason endlessly, and argue over consequences, on such matters as the balance of trade or the impact of various taxes; but since Political Economy in England, Germany, and France has been founded in observation of everyday facts there is agreement on basic essentials. All leading writers in this science now maintain, for example, that gold and silver are not the only values, and that wealth is both formed and destroyed. We know for what purpose, and in how many ways, capital is employed in the act of production, etc. Those who are unaware of how many positively established ideas exist on these matters are not really abreast of the science of our time.

It is from not employing such ideas as a guide to practice that we see in France, perhaps more than elsewhere, so much eagerness to launch into enterprises that have no chance of success, and to reject procedures that then go to enrich foreign countries. We find people enthusiastic for a project before bringing the necessary elements into their calculations; they hazard their fortunes and the fortunes of their families on some vague and incomplete impression; they spend much time, money, labor, and even science on a product that is not worth what is put into it. . . .

An improvement in manufacturing processes certainly produces savings in some costs of production, but these savings have their limits; they should not pass certain bounds, and should not be paid for beyond what they are worth. Another improvement multiplies products with surprising speed, but the consumption of the product has its limits, and nothing is to be gained by exceeding the limits of possible consumption, however ingenious the process of production may be. It is only Political Economy that indicates the elements, and the *totality of elements*, that must be brought into various calculations. You know, Monsieur, that the only sound judgments are those that consider the totality of factors that may influence the results.

How many mistaken ideas, and false notions of the nature of things that concern them, do we not find among the class of merchants and manufacturers? And how many conversations that reveal their lack of instruction? They hardly know the value of the words they use. They attribute commercial events to irrelevant causes, and foresee results that are not in the order of things possible. Those of us who have traveled in England have observed, as I have (let us speak in confidence to each other) that in this respect the British are far more advanced.

Here Say puts in a footnote, noting that manufacturers especially in Scotland are successful because they make judicious use of the means of production, in part because political economy is taught at Edinburgh and Glasgow, and has been taught there since Adam Smith, "the father of modern political economy as now taught." The main text continues:

Hence badly conceived enterprises, bad methods of execution, and unsuccessful results are less frequent than in France. There are fewer establishments that vegetate or decline, and it must be admitted that an appearance of well-being is more general than in France, despite the burden of taxes to which industry in England is subjected. Our problem in France then is to get rid of many prejudices standing in the way of good judgment on questions of industry, to make more widely known ideas that are common elsewhere, and have manufacturers who are more than superior workmen. This increment is indispensable if we are to become a truly manufacturing nation. . . .

To stimulate the entrepreneurial spirit without enlightening it is harmful to public prosperity. To educate hard-working men in manufacturing processes and induce the employment of capital, without showing the conditions indispensable for making these resources bear fruit in their hands, is to lay them a trap. The sciences can yield admirable products to prove how far the human intelligence can go; but unless industrial economy is consulted they can do nothing for human well-being, which is to say happiness. Let other institutions restrict themselves, at the expense of the State, to offering fine collections to public curiosity. An institution priding itself on educating for utility should show, in addition, how utility is produced.

Such are the considerations, Monsieur, that deserve being brought to the attention of the committee charged with making the Conservatory of Arts and Trade into the first establishment of this kind in Europe. From my correspondence with men in our principal cities, I have reason to think that the committee will do itself much honor by taking the initiative in an improvement that in one way or another will take place in coming years. I reach this judgment from the great movement now occurring in this order of ideas, of which I have been made aware by my correspondents.

The new course at the Conservatory opened late in 1820, and Say delivered his introductory lecture on December 2 to a mixed but sizeable audience. He addressed his hearers as if they were a group of entrepreneurs, although how many actually were such is unknown. Repeating much of what he had said to Thénard, he told them that it was not enough to understand the technology of production, and that political economy was a true science by which they might be helped in their business. In conclusion, he urged them to feel no guilt in pursuing their own self-interest (the profit motive so frowned on in many quarters), since to do so in the right way was also to be useful to others, and hence moral.

Messieurs:

The government shows its commendable concern for the progress of the useful arts by establishing the course in which you are about to take part at the Conservatory for Arts and Trades. This institution is without model in the other states of Europe, where it deserves to be imitated. There exist everywhere chairs for the teaching of letters, medicine, and law, and in some countries for the physical and mathematical sciences. There are even courses in technology, or the practice of the arts, but until now nothing has been done, in the way of public establishments, to enable persons engaged in industrial occupations to benefit from the advance of knowledge on which our age justly prides itself. . . .

It is time, therefore, to provide a kind of instruction in which, without cost, men engaged in industrial labors may share in the findings of scholars; an instruction which from one year to the next may keep them abreast of the latest state of the sciences, allow discoveries in one of the arts to be made known to the others, and generalize procedures which for lack of a common center might remain buried in some remote part of the kingdom. . . .

Have we not too often seen intelligent and assiduous men, who understand the theory and practice of the arts, nevertheless struggle against fortune without success, multiply their sacrifices to sustain enterprises that ought to succumb, and lose not only their own capital but also sometimes the capital entrusted to them by others?

It may be that the usefulness of a hydraulic engine has been exaggerated and its costs wrongly accounted for. The water power has been employed with the least possible loss, and all transmissions of motion made consistent with the soundest ideas in mechanics. What was also necessary, however, was to calculate how much value this natural source of power would add to the resulting product, to know whether the value produced might be less than the cost of bringing workers to the site of the engine, and of training and housing them; or whether the transport of raw materials to the location of the factory, or of products to the place of consumption, might not cost more than the savings to be gained by use of the motive power.

Or there may be a manufacturer who is too confident in his own complete knowledge of his art and seduced by his previous successes, and so ruins himself by not having appreciated the difference in places and circumstances, or by wrongly estimating the competition of another product, or by failing to reflect on the population, customs, and prejudices of the places where consumers are to be found.

Hence there may be distrust on the part of possessors of capital when it is a question of advances for industrial enterprise. Or an exaggerated confidence may be equally harmful, when it is not realized that the honesty, activity, and talent of entrepreneurs are not sufficient guarantees of success. Brilliant but chimerical expectations may be seductive, and the most extravagant ideas find support and win public favor, while more commendable arts languish indefinitely, until transported to foreign countries where they flourish and show us the harvest of wealth that we have neglected.

It is to avoid these failings (so far as human wisdom can flatter itself on doing so) that the useful arts taught at the Conservatory of Arts and Trades are to include not only applied chemistry and mechanics but also *Industrial Economy.*

He goes on at some length to explain that political economy is a science, often using the same words as in the letter to Trénard and indeed since the first edition of his *Treatise.* We have already seen what he means by "experimental."

The method that I have described, and which in modern times has so remarkably contributed to the progress of the sciences, may be called the experimental method. It is this method, when applied to Political Economy [not "industrial" here] that has placed it in the rank of the experimental sciences; but I must first call your attention to the experiences that serve as its base.

These experiences take much time and can almost never be repeated at will. When a physicist tells you that bodies fall with increasing speed according to a law of acceleration, he can bring this as a fact of experience before your eyes; you can repeat it yourself if you are curious to study the circumstances and know it under different conditions. But when a political economist tells you that the division of labor, or separation of occupations among several classes of workers, augments the productive power of industry in certain proportions, he cannot bring to you and put before your eyes a number of productive establishments, set them going, and wait with you to see the results of their operation or measure them in your presence. His experiments, or rather his experience, are the result of all the observations that he has been able to make whenever the world has presented a circumstance from which a consequence could be drawn, so as to know either the nature of things or the connection between the facts. He then tells you what he has observed; and it is for you to recall analogous cases where you have been able to make observations yourself. Or you can lie in wait, so to speak, for circumstances that will present themselves in the future, and then draw the consequences that the professor will have taught you how to draw.

You will even be able, more than once in your career and whatever your business, to make good use of his instruction when you see some advantage, and apply your experiences of several years to what you will perceive in five minutes.

In some of the most positive sciences experiments cannot be made and repeated as we choose—in astronomy, for example. Can we make the slightest astronomical phenomenon come to pass? Yet the distance, motion, and even the mass of several planets are among the best-established facts; we know the rotation of the sun and the speed of light; we have calculated revolutions that take 25,000 years to complete. Although it is hardly two hundred years since we have been able to make fairly exact observations, we have obtained on these points such a degree of certainty that there is now no tolerably educated person anywhere in the world who does not accept the reality of these findings, and apply them in practice whenever the occasion arises.

It is the same, Messieurs, with experimental Political Economy, the only one that I shall present to you, although in general we cannot repeat experiences at will. Nevertheless, the facts that are the basis of political economy occur so often in the ordinary course of life that anyone whose attention has been awakened by previous instruction can often repeat his observations and enjoy almost the same advantages as the chemist or physicist who can bring bodies into contact and observe the results whenever they think it appropriate. . . .

But we do not ask of any study more than it can promise. Industrial economy will tell you how wealth is formed and distributed, but if you wish to produce wealth it is not enough to know this science; you must practice its precepts. It does not give you the instruments for making your fortune, but it tells you what these instruments are. That is not everything, but it is something.

Mechanics and chemistry show you what you *can do*. Industrial economy shows what you *had best do*. The problem is to overcome difficulties, not all difficulties indiscriminately, but those that can be overcome with advantage. Only economic knowledge can give you the certain signs for making the distinction. . . .

While severe moralists reproach men in vain for listening only to their own interest, let us show them what a rightly understood interest is. Let us prove to them that, although in some particular cases bad men have profited from crimes and injustice, yet on the whole the gain to be enjoyed most securely, most peacefully, and for the longest time, is the *gain properly acquired*. This form of acquisition is always the most favorable to society; it is one of the truths that appear most often in a study of the methods and results of industry. . . .

May these thoughts, Messieurs, strengthen you in your noble resolution to be useful to society by the very efforts that make you useful to yourselves. Be assured that when active in industry you will be working at the same time for morality and happiness, for the public as well as the private good.

Say continued to lecture at the Conservatory of Arts and Trades for ten years, always drawing a sizeable audience. Presumably expounding only "industrial economy," he avoided overt comment on current political questions, and the government never closed his course, as it did those offered at the Sorbonne by François Guizot and Victor Cousin in these years. He invited his hearers to submit written questions on points they found hard to understand, and in a later lecture would try to elucidate them. There were moments when he doubted the success of his efforts. He remarked in a letter to Ricardo in 1822:

Our nation, absorbed in business, pleasure, and political quarrels, gives very little attention to economic questions. Hence the progress of instruction on this subject is slow. Twice a week I develop a few elementary principles, concerning only practical application, in a fine hall prepared for me by the government at the Conservatory of Arts and Trades; and I observe, to the shame of our nation, that half my audience is composed of foreigners, Englishmen, Russians, Poles, Germans, Spaniards, Portuguese, and Greeks. The hereditary prince of Denmark, soon to depart for London and unable to finish the course, has requested me to initiate him privately in the principles of political economy, which he seems to have grasped very well—a good augury for the peoples he will have to govern.

To spread his message more widely, he published in 1828 a *Cours complet d'économie politique pratique*, in which his spoken lectures were apparently amplified, since the "complete course" ran to seven volumes. Its long subtitle stated its aim: "a work intended to bring social economy (*l'économie des sociétés*) to the attention of statesmen, property owners and capitalists, scholars, farmers, manufacturers, merchants, and in general all citizens." Despite its length it was several times reprinted in French, and it soon appeared in German and Italian, though never in English.

His *Treatise on Political Economy* did appear somewhat tardily in English in 1821, but he was unhappy with the translation and the translator, Robert Prinsep, to whom he wrote on receipt of the book. He thanked him for the honor done to his *Treatise*, "since English is the only European language in which it had not yet been printed." This was an exaggeration, but it had in fact been translated before 1821 at least into German, Italian, Spanish, Swedish, and Danish.

Writing to Prinsep, he raised various matters on which they disagreed, such as paper money, the money supply, inflation, and utility, but he especially objected to Prinsep's omission of his Introduction, from which selections are given in chapter 3 of this volume.

> . . . As for your translation, Monsieur, it seems to me to have been made conscientiously with a sincere desire to propagate economic knowledge. But I would have wished you to include the Introduction with which the work begins and the Epitome with which it ends. I know not why you have supposed that a preamble setting forth the purpose of political economy, answering objections raised against it as a field of knowledge, showing its advantages to mankind, and giving a brief history of its progress, should be without interest for readers of a book on this subject. Professors using it as a text in Italy, Germany, Poland, Russia, Sweden, and Holland have not shared in your opinion.

He might have added that when Prinsep's translation was brought out in Philadelphia the American editor, Clement Biddle, made somewhat the same criticisms, and translated and incorporated Say's Introduction.

Say became even more caustic on Prinsep's notes and comments accompanying his translation.

I pass over many other of your notes in which you give me lessons, perhaps too pompously, on how I should have treated my subject. See especially your notes on page 488 of volume I and pages 20, 70, and 89 of volume II. And what are your arguments in support of your advice? Most often they reduce themselves to this: "You say *yes* and I say *no*; and you are undoubtedly wrong because I am right." It seems to me that before putting your view of economic questions in place of mine, and judging so authoritatively, you should have proved to the reader that you are older than I am, and that in making your translation you had reflected more fully than an author who had worked on the book for twenty years.

What is annoying is that you seem so satisfied with your own ideas as to think it useless to try to comprehend mine. This is evident especially in the first chapters of Book II, which I regret to say you have not understood at all, from failing to see the point of view of the author. How can the English understand an interpreter who by his own admission has not understood the original?

What makes me suppose that your notes are somewhat carelessly written is not only your promptness in condemnation before sufficient reflection, but in asserting facts that can easily be seen as false, as when you attribute to me the French translation of Ricardo, although this translation is not mine and carries the name of its translator, M. Constancio, in plain letters.

The same carelessness is revealed in your note to page 239 of the first volume, where you suppose that I treat Napoleon severely because I received some *provocation* from him. I assure you, Monsieur, that I received no personal provocation from him whatsoever. He even offered me a lucrative post in the public service, and it was I who sent in my resignation when he became emperor, not wishing to share with him in the spoliation of France.

The remainder of this letter to Prinsep is a long diatribe against Napoleon, declaring that he had outrageously abused an opportunity open to him in 1800, and gone on to violate all decent possibilities and expectations.

This letter to Prinsep was not known in Say's lifetime, but in his role as the leading economist in France he made public his observations on various other contemporaries. For example, he wrote a brief review of a work by the American publicist Matthew Carey, questioning the wisdom of Carey's approval of protective tariffs. As already noted, he published his letters to Malthus, supplied notes to the French translation of Ricardo, and wrote an article on Sismondi concerning overproduction, the balance of production and consumption, and what later came to be known as Say's Law. Of interest also are his notes to a French edition of a work on political economy by Heinrich Storch, published in St. Petersburg in 1815 (in French, so that no translation was in question), and in Paris in 1823. By invitation from the French publisher Say supplemented the Paris edition of Storch's book with copious annotations, many of which were on fine points in economics, but many were also of more general interest. One of these, excerpted in chapter 4 of this book, clarified Say's conception of the entrepreneur. Two others deserve inclusion here: one on the historical connection between commerce and liberty, and one on the nature of civilization.

He attributes the growth of liberty more to a commercial bourgeoisie than to landed proprietors. His glance at English history is therefore inexact, except insofar as influential landowners in England had become more "commercial" themselves.

> An important consequence can be deduced from the parallel that M. Storch, following Adam Smith, traces between commercial and agricultural wealth.
>
> Although capital invested in the improvement of land produces more solidly acquired wealth for a nation, or at least a wealth that deteriorates less than the immense capital that gives life to commercial towns, on the other hand such improvements of land offer an encouragement to bad government and arbitrary power. A landowner, especially when he has made his land highly productive, is always vulnerable to authority; he cannot escape it. The landowner cannot pick up his field and take it away; like a slave, he is attached to the soil, obliged to bear the yoke of government whether it be light or heavy. The capitalist or merchant, on the contrary, can send funds elsewhere, and follow them if necessary. Independence of their persons gives them independence of thought; it is here that we find more dignity and true patriotism; and authority is in general obliged to deal with them carefully, or at least with justice. The tax collector can ravage land, which is always there to yield tribute, while capital and industry depart when exactions become excessive, and the tax authorities, so as not to lose all, are obliged to moderate their rapacity.
>
> So we see that despotic states are almost always agricultural states, such as China, India, and Egypt. In Europe, France, being almost purely agricultural until the eighteenth century, was unable to establish its liberty, while England, in proportion as it became more commercial, could constantly win its rights, obtain fair law courts and the freedom of the press that prevents all the great injustices.

As for civilization, Say and Storch were agreed that it was a good thing, but they differed on what it consisted in, or the signs by which it might be known. Storch identified it with an economic category of what he called "internal goods," as distinct from external objects, while for

Say it consisted in, and could be seen in, the production and consumption of whatever supplied human needs and enjoyments.

Since Storch persistently confuses civilization with internal goods, it must first be seen in what ways this equivalence is defective. Internal goods, as he lists them, are health, skill, understanding, taste, morals, religion, security, and leisure. (See his p. 330.) It is the possession of these goods, he thinks, that characterizes civilization; but who would imagine that Voltaire lacked civilization because he had poor health, or that Maréchal de Richelieu, so brilliant in the reign of Louis XV, was uncivilized because he had detestable morals, or that the society of Ninon de l'Enclos, Mme. du Deffand, or Frederick II, though composed of the most distinguished men of their time, was not composed of civilized people because they had the misfortune of not going to confession or fasting during Lent?

We must therefore look for other traits of civilization. . . .

The word "civilization" is new in French, but whatever its origin no one would deny, I think not even M. Storch, that it always evokes the idea of a certain development of human physical and moral faculties. One nation is more civilized than another simply insofar as human faculties have obtained a greater development, a development that can take place only in a social state for reasons that I cannot explain here.

Now our faculties are of two kinds: we have the ability to act, and the ability to enjoy; to create products and to consume them. Civilization will be the greater, the more is produced and the more consumed, the more there are needs and the more they are provided for. What do we have beyond the Kalmucks? Only that we produce and consume more.

The same remark can be made on the grosser and more developed parts of the same nation. The comfortable inhabitant of one of our large towns is more developed than the peasant of Lower Brittany because he feels the need for more delicate food and more refinements in clothing and lodging, is able to appreciate reading and enjoy products of the fine arts, etc., and seeks to satisfy these needs by producing, either by his personal abilities or by use of his capital and lands, the things suitable to meet these needs, or at least the means of acquiring them. . . .

If the preceding gives a correct idea of civilization we should conclude that the social circumstances favoring it are those that tend to develop the taste and need for well-understood enjoyments, and to discover the best means of satisfying them. I say *well understood enjoyments*, for without this condition our ability to enjoy cannot reach its highest level; and I say *best means of satisfying them* because, without this condition, our ability to produce cannot reach such a level either. . . .

Finally, we must not take as an end what should be regarded only as a means. A people is not civilized because it enjoys security. There is great security in Lapland, for according to travelers there are rarely locks to be seen on the doors of houses, and there is no exposure to tax-collectors or police spies; and yet no one can say that the Lapps are civilized. Security then in itself does not constitute civilization. We must be content to say that security is a necessary prerequisite for a nation to become completely civilized.

These notes added by Say to Storch's book on political economy, some of which may indeed have been unfair to him, provoked a reply which Storch published in Paris. Storch counterattacked by accusing Say of violating Storch's property rights for his own profit. Say responded in a letter to the editors of the *Révue encyclopédique*. Here, besides reaffirming his own ideas in economics, he accused Storch of palpable plagiarism: "Three-quarters of his book is copied textually from the works of Adam Smith (in Garnier's translation), Jeremy Bentham, Sismondi, Destutt de Tracy, and myself. He has used my work so freely that I have found in his book whole chapters of my *Treatise on Political Economy*, from the first to the last word, including the chapter titles!"

No rebuttal by Storch is recorded.

The years of Say's lifetime coincided with the height of the canal age, for he had been born in 1767 while the pioneering Liverpool and Manchester Canal was under construction, and two years before his death the equally memorable Liverpool and Manchester Railway inaugurated a revolution in transportation. In America, the famous Erie Canal began operations in 1825. Only two years later the Mohawk and Hudson Railroad was chartered, the first segment of what would become the New York Central, which by paralleling the Erie Canal eventually put it out of business.

Say himself thought that canals might be supplemented by some kind of improved land transportation. It may be recalled that he saw "ambulant steam engines" in Yorkshire in 1814. Even before this visit to England he made a curious prediction of the coming of the railroad in a footnote to the second edition of the *Treatise* in 1814. It occurs where he mentions canals along with roads and docks as public works that governments should promote. In this footnote the contrivance that he has in mind is called *coulisses de fonte*, which may be translated as cast-iron grooves, on which experiments were being made before the adoption of the upright rail. The note was repeated in later editions of the *Treatise*, but was very imperfectly translated in the English edition of 1821. Here is a more satisfactory version of what he said in 1814 and later editions of the *Treatise*:

For lack of canals it is probable that cast-iron grooves will eventually be established for communication from one town to another. However costly their first construction might be, it is probable that the resulting economy in transportation would more than pay the interest on the first advances. These cast-iron grooves, set in masonry, would have the advantage, in addition to easing the movement of wheeled vehicles, of not jostling the passengers and merchandise. These huge enterprises are being undertaken in countries [no doubt England] that have the large amounts of capital needed for the considerable advances, and where the government inspires enough confidence for entrepreneurs not to fear losing the fruit of their investment.

In the *Treatise* he mentioned canals only in passing, but he discussed them at some length in two places, once in 1818 in a pamphlet on canals in general with special reference to Paris, and again a few years later on the Erie Canal in the United States. He wrote in 1818:

There is now much interest in canals among many other objects of public utility. But does everyone understand how and to what extent canals promote the wealth of a nation? I should like to take the doubters to the gorges of the Jura, or to the Auvergne or the Pyrenees, and show them trees a hundred feet tall that are not worth a hundred sous, or that have no value at all since their owners let them die in place. I would then show them these same trees, or the boards made from them, brought by easy transportation to the quays of a large town, where they acquire a value by furnishing new products for the needs of industry and consumption.

Applying this example to all cases of production and consumption, we shall have the key to the advantages of communication by sea, improved roads, and canals which are only a kind of improved roads. We have values where none existed, or an increase of values that existed already, and an augmentation of products in favor of the consumer. Then all parts of a country can make good use of their means of production. Grain can then be produced with confidence in the Beauce, wines in Champagne, oysters at Cancale, and patés at Amiens. The cost of transporting all these products to Paris does not absorb their whole value, and Paris pays for them with furniture, women's shawls, books—who can number the immensity of its products?

Progress in commercial industry, as in other industries, consists in obtaining the same benefits at less cost, or what is the same thing, greater benefits at the same cost. Products become less dear, and so are more widely consumed and more actively multiplied. Transport by wheeled vehicles is a limited and costly means of communicating unsuited to an advanced state of commercial communication and supply.

Internal navigation should in most cases replace the wheel, as the wheel replaced transport by mule-back. A beast of burden carries two or three hundredweight on its back; attached to a wagon it pulls fifteen or eighteen; when attached to boats it can pull more than sixty.

In a word, all means of communication are good in multiplying the values that constitute wealth; but among means of communication the best are canals. . . .

The great rivers of France are far from being as useful as they might be for commercial communications. One can, if one wants to, transport merchandise from Nantes to Paris by water. This route is avoided whenever possible. Although the Seine offers the most direct communication from Rouen to Paris, wheeled vehicles are still preferred. Use of rivers is too often impeded unless they have canals which shorten some of their bends, or which run alongside of them, and on which boats can find sufficient water without current in all seasons so as to glide equally well in both directions.

In any case, even when rivers are navigable at all times, there must be artificial means of passing from one river basin to another. This comes with canals at watersheds through the use of locks. . . .

M. Girard, in an excellent paper read at the Academy of Sciences, observed that the progress of internal navigation has been in inverse ratio to the size of canals. The ancients wanted to make seagoing ships pass from the Red Sea to the Mediterranean, and from the Black Sea to the Caspian. It appears that they failed. When locks were invented in the fifteenth century the size of canals was reduced to the size needed to transport river boats from one river bed to another. It was on this plan that the Briare canal was dug under Henry IV, and the Canal du Midi under Louis XIV, honorable monuments to the reigns of these princes, and the French genius.

He turns next to a more recent improvement, the use of barges, for which he seems to have no word, and which he attributes to the enterprise of the English.

One last step remained to be taken; it was to make canals simply into fluid roads on which it was possible to impart easy movement, without jostling or clashing, to long rectangular boxes that would hardly deserve the name of boats, but which when chained to each other and accommodating to the sinuosities in the route, like the coils of a snake, were enough for all kinds of transportation and for the busiest commerce. It was the English who did this. The duke of Bridgewater, about 1758, had the idea of making navigable the discharges of exhausted water from his coal mines near Manchester. He built a canal parallel to the river Mersey to communicate with Liverpool and bring products available in that seaport. He was successful; and nothing is as contagious as success. Since that time canals, having become less costly and covering less space, have so greatly multiplied on the surface of England that their total length today exceeds *two thousand leagues.* . . .

.   Such are the means of communication that France needs today. It needs them even more than England, for it is not compensated, as England is, for difficulties in internal communication by a considerable development of its seacoast, not having a heavily indented coastline by which the sea reaches into the heart of the country. The coal of Newcastle and Lancashire can arrive at London by sea. Could we do likewise with the coal of Saint-Etienne and Valenciennes? Let us then be thankful to those patriotic capitalists who are turning their attention to these useful speculations. May they find, under a protective government, in the products of their enterprise and in public approbation, a just reward for their sacrifices!

While all the provinces of France need navigable canals, Paris and its environs need them more than any other place. Paris is very different from what it was before the Revolution. The passing of huge buildings from the hands of the priesthood to those of industry, the investment of capital in trade because squandering it no longer confers honor, an activity of mind, the ordinary result of civil discords, leading on to ways of independence and fortune, the astonishing progress in application of sciences to the arts, all these causes and many others have in the last twenty-five years made Paris one of the most important centers of manufacture in the world.

The rest of Say's article on canals is devoted to plans for connecting the Marne, Seine, and Oise rivers at a point then on the outskirts of Paris, at La Villette. The government was already at work on this undertaking, with various interruptions and delays, so that Say urged that the work be accomplished by more cooperation between government bodies and private capitalists and entrepreneurs.

When Say wrote this article, construction had already begun on the Erie Canal. In 1821 the government of New York State published a collection of documents concerning these operations, of which a copy reached the *Revue encyclopédique.* Say, now a frequent contributor to this journal, promptly reviewed it in January 1822. He praised the speed with which work on the Erie Canal was going forward, although it was a project of the state rather than private enterprise, and he saw its future importance, even noting that steamboats might use it where he had made no mention of steamboats for internal navigation in France. One element of future importance eluded him. Stressing the future connection between New York and New Orleans by internal waterways including the Ohio River, he did not foresee that the Erie Canal would make possible a massive migration into the upper Middle West. Nor did he anticipate the coming of railroads, as he had done in the footnote to his *Treatise*.

As he explained it to the French and indeed international audience of the *Revue encyclopédique*:

> The United States of America were at first only a nation extending along the coasts of a vast continent covered with forests. Now that they have pushed their settlements to the Mississippi they form a vast empire almost as wide as long, and mainly agricultural. But the eastern and western parts of this empire communicate with difficulty; they are separated by the chain of the Alleghenies, which intercepts all navigation between the waters emptying into the ocean and those flowing into the Mississippi.
>
> The necessary relations between the two halves of so large a country have brought about, by land, an active communication between Philadelphia on the ocean and Pittsburgh on the Ohio, at the point where this river becomes easily navigable. But, to give an idea of the difficulty in this mountainous connection by land, though it is the shortest possible between east and west, it burdens the transported merchandise with a cost of at least 30 francs per hundred pounds of weight. Almost no agricultural product can support such an expense, so that the products of half the states in the Union must find their outlet by way of the Mississippi and New Orleans, and obtain returning goods by the same route.
>
> Internal navigation can and soon will join the two halves of the American confederation. The Alleghenies that separate them become lower and disappear as they approach the immense lakes that flow into the St. Lawrence River. Hence a canal can be opened running from the Hudson River near Albany to Lake Erie. Then, by a canal only two leagues long [six miles] which presents no difficulty, Lake Erie can communicate with the Cuyahoga, Muskingum, and Ohio rivers. The Ohio is the great artery of the west.
>
> The execution of this plan has been pursued with such vigor and effectiveness that a project whose completion seemed to require twelve or fifteen years will be finished in less than six. The essential part, establishing contact between New York City and Lake Erie, began in 1817 and will be completed in 1823.
>
> The purpose of the volume we have before us is to make known the difficulties to be faced before adoption of the plan, and then in its implementation. The most important piece in the collection is a report, first published in 1816 in the name of the people of New York, pre-

pared by M. Clinton, the present governor, that is the head of the executive power of New York State. Well thought out and well written, it explains first of all the salutary influence of communications at little expense between all parts of the country, and the superiority of *liquid roads*, as canals are called, over any other means of communication. These principles, founded on the most recent and soundest ideas of political economy, are applied to an examination of the project that we have just described, and the author deduces from them the probable results, all of them important for the confederation in general, and for the state of New York in particular.

This excellent report led to the appointment of a commission, which took the trouble to traverse the 160 leagues over which the Erie Canal would have to pass. Specifications were drawn up, mile by mile, with costs of construction according to varying features of the terrain, and it was only after a thorough investigation that the state of New York adopted the project and put it into execution. When such precautions are taken before an enterprise is begun, and then observed so carefully when it is launched, there is good reason to count on success. The present volume, which may be a model for all peoples eager to establish an internal navigation, is accompanied by a magnificent topographic map of places through which the canal must pass, with profiles showing the various elevations. We presume, from what we have read here, that within three years a steamboat will be able to leave New York, pass from the Hudson River into Lake Erie, gain the Ohio, and reach New Orleans by descending the Mississippi.

Another document from America also reached the editors of the *Revue encyclopédique*: the seventh annual report of the American Colonization Society, published in 1824. It concerned what became the African state of Liberia, and Say reviewed it. "Colonization," or the sending of free blacks in the United States back to Africa, was widely favored at this time when both the abolition of slavery and interracial harmony seemed impossible. Thomas Jefferson and Alexis de Tocqueville spoke well of it, and Daniel Webster and Henry Clay were listed among the Society's seventeen vice-presidents. Even whites most sympathetic to blacks believed that they might live more comfortably in Africa. Some even hoped that a colony of blacks who had acquired traits of civilization in America would help to civilize the rest of the African continent. But the idea was impractical if only because free blacks in the United States were too numerous for such a displacement, and very few of them wanted to go back to Africa anyway.

Say's article was entitled "on the first colony formed by the Americans in Africa." He called the blacks simply "Americans," as perhaps few whites in the United States would then have done. His comments on use of the word "American" in various languages are also of interest. He began:

In the opinion of the most enlightened persons in the United States the part of their population composed of blacks and people of color is a canker that may be fatal to their great republic, and is to a certain extent contrary to the rising prosperity promoted by all its other institutions. Slavery is nonsense in a nation that regards all men as equal, a nation that honors labor, and where all political powers come from the people and have no object except the general welfare. . . .

The relative degree of suffering of some inhabitants of the country, as compared with others, can only lead to dangerous crises. Nor is it to be supposed that the disease affects only the Negro slaves. The free blacks and persons of color are themselves afflicted by an inescapable disapproval, as unavoidable as the nuance in the color of their skin. In vain do liberal institutions in the United States open the way to careers for them; almost none are to be found in the most respected positions in society. From childhood the colored person is the butt of sarcasms from schoolmates; he feels scorned before he can know why, and is punished before being guilty. The free black senses himself to be of a species from which slaves are made, as the white person never is. It is impossible that a man condemned by his appearance to general disdain should have the self-esteem of one who enjoys public consideration. Even if his soul feels no degradation, how can he avoid at least a sense of irritation against society? . . .

Such considerations led several good citizens to form an association, at Washington in 1817, to lay the basis and promote development on the coast of Africa of a colony composed mainly of free blacks and people of color, who, already possessing the habits and arts of civilized living, might diffuse them through these still savage countries, and become in time the nucleus of a great state to receive a colored population that finds its existence too painful in the United States or any other country peopled by whites. A chain of civilized colonies on the coast of Africa would open up commercial and maritime relations between two worlds, and would end forever the frightful trade in human flesh that still disgraces certain nations, or at least some greedy speculators who are impervious to both humanity and shame.

He goes on to summarize how the Colonization Society sent two of its agents to Africa to locate a place for settlement, with the encouragement of the United States government, since the laws against importation of slaves were being violated by smugglers, and slaves thus brought illegally into the United States.

The government therefore decided to favor the project for colonization in order to have a place on the African coast as a base for cruisers, which could take possession of slave-trading ships, confiscate the captured slaves, and deposit them on the African coast. The society sent out the *Elizabeth* with about 80 colored colonists, who would initiate the settlement under command of two commissioners from the government and one from the Society.

But the place chosen proved unsatisfactory; there was resistance from native Africans, the three commissioners and twenty colonists took sick and died; more commissioners and twenty-eight more colonists arrived; more disorders followed, and all took refuge in the neighboring British colony of Sierra Leone.

But one commissioner from the Society and one from the government survived, and finally succeeded in purchasing for 300 piasters, on the banks of a fine river, near Cape Montserado, an extremely favorable location, on high ground, of sufficient extent, healthful, fertile, and provided with an excellent natural harbor. After much negotiation a treaty was concluded and ratified, and the settlement began. But treaties that suit a country do not always suit those in the country who live by corruption. Some bad advisers, some of them suspected of being agents of European slave traders, persuaded the rulers and chiefs of the neighboring region that a colony founded on liberal principles would endanger their power and profits; they understood that consolidation of the colony would result in suppression of the slave trade, that is, the traffic in the blood of their subjects, which these black princes carried on in imitation of their confreres of another color. The colonists, facing such hostility, were obliged to work with a spade in one hand and a musket in the other.

In the midst of these difficulties an accident caused the warehouse to take fire; almost all provisions, clothing, and military supplies were consumed by the flames. The situation of the colony became desperate. Hordes from the neighborhood prepared a decisive attack to annihilate the Americans. Fortunately the Society had already succeeded in sending a new brig loaded with provisions and thirty-five new colonists. It also brought fifteen Negroes liberated by capture of a slave trading ship, who felt the most lively gratitude for their liberators. This expedition was led by Mr. Ashmun, who was accompanied by his wife, and was authorized to take command in the colony if necessary. He built some fortifications, and toward the end of 1821 had to sustain two attacks in which, thanks to a few artillery pieces, he repelled 800 assailants on the first occasion, and 1,500 on the second.

Despite these successes and the great preponderance of civilization over barbarism, the situation in the colony was far from reassuring, when a British ship, the *Cyane*, engaged in enforcing laws against the slave trade, arrived. Its captain and crew showed great zeal in defense of the new settlement; they helped in building a stone fort and a good house for the agent of the Society.

After much more on the troubles of the colony, Say goes on to tell how it received its name, at the seventh annual meeting of the Society in Washington in 1824.

> In the general assembly of the Society a member proposed to give a name to the new colony at Cape Monserado. The influence of names is greater than one imagines. Ideas are not fixed on a thing, place, or nation unless people know what to call it. . . . The United States suffer at present from having only a name that might suit any federation having a common bond, such as Switzerland, or Greece if its present efforts at renewal are successful. But how can we speak without paraphrase of a citizen of the United States as we speak of an Englishman or a Frenchman? It is the country with the most citizens and the fewest words to designate them. The English, indeed, reserve the word "American" for them exclusively, and call the people of the Antilles "West Indians," but as long as the New World is America it will be impossible not to call Americans all people from Cape Horn to Hudson Bay. Such is the usage of all the languages of Europe, except English.
>
> Probably such considerations led General Harper to propose in the assembly of the Society the name *Liberia* for the territory of the colony, whatever its future extent may be, and *Monrovia* for the town still in its infancy that will become its capital. The first of these names, he explained, is a reminder of the purpose for which the colony was established, to provide an asylum for those who from serfs became free men. The second offers deserved homage to the president of the United States, *James Monroe*, whose enlightened zeal has so well served the cause of his country and of all humanity.

At the end of this article on Liberia Say gave a cross reference to later pages in the same number of the *Revue encyclopédique*, containing information that apparently reached the *Revue* too late for Say to incorporate it into his discussion of American efforts in Africa. It was highly relevant to that subject, for it suggested another place that might be better than Africa for resettlement of American blacks—namely, Haiti. That Americans should go to Haiti to enjoy freedom, rather than Haitians fleeing to the United States as in the 1990s, may seem as startling an irony to readers of this book as to its author.

An officer of the American Colonization Society, probably in view of its years of trouble in Africa, wrote in 1824 to the president of the Republic of Haiti, Jean-Pierre Boyer, to ask in detail on what terms Haiti would receive American blacks. Boyer was chief of state in Haiti from 1818 to 1843, and his regime is remembered as a long period of relative peace in the history of that unfortunate island. He replied to the American inquiry in a letter of almost two thousand words, in which he praised the Society for its good intentions but expressed dislike for sending American blacks back to Africa. "The project of sending men accustomed to civilization as colonists to regions that are barbarous, so to speak, has seemed to me to be impracticable." He assured the Society that American blacks would be received in Haiti "with pleasure," and would enjoy the rights and liberties provided by the Haitian constitution. They would be granted good land for agriculture, and encouragement in the arts and trades. *"Enfin, Monsieur"* (for of course the president of Haiti wrote in French), "to prove how far I am willing to assist our unfortunate brothers who still groan in the United States under old prejudices (of which Blacks have long been victims) I am about to send to New York both funds and a confidential agent empowered to negotiate with you and your Society. . . ." He would also accept American blacks returning from Liberia. "There could be no better opportunity," he said, "to offer an agreeable hospitality and secure asylum to unfortunates exposed to suffering and death on the coasts of Africa."

Nothing came of this exchange of letters, probably from disapproval in the United States. It must be remembered that the existence of slavery in the United States prevented its recognition of the Haitian Republic until 1861.

Of more practical value for readers of the *Revue encyclopédique* was an article contributed by Say in 1827 on statistics. It was a time of transition for statistics from its earlier to more modern form. "Political arithmetic" had been known in England since the seventeenth century, but the word "statistics" originated in mid-eighteenth-century Germany, from which it passed into English and French somewhat later. There was uncertainty as to what it meant; it referred to matters of concern to the state, and especially to the collection of numerical data, but it might also include verbal descriptions of a country's climate, resources, products, and people. Say wrote in order to clarify this uncertainty, and may have contributed to the transition then under way; the ancestor of the French *Annuaire statistique*, or statistical yearbook, first appeared in 1835.

He could not foresee the length to which statistical analysis would eventually go in elaboration of mathematical formulas, and in application to the physical as well as the social sciences, to archaeology and linguistics, and to market research, party politics, polling, and studies of public opinion. But he touched on various perennial methodological issues, such as the importance of establishing trends in time, the significance of numerical correlation, the determination of cause and effect, and the means of collecting and credibility of the original data. Most especially, he saw the value of statistics not merely in knowledge for its own sake but in knowledge as a means of social improvement.

His article, entitled "On the object and utility of statistics," began as follows:

> Everyone knows that the purpose of statistics is to make known the social situation of a country, province, or town at a given moment. Many writers include a physical description of a country, its mountains, valleys, and irregularities of terrain, including the rivers that water it and the seas that bathe its shores. It is evident that such features are subjects for *physical geography* and not for *statistics*. For this latter science the problem is to present not changeless things but those that can change in time. This is also the basis of the true importance of statistics, for man can improve bad social institutions, but he cannot rid himself of a rigorous climate or a sterile soil, or at least his power in this respect is very limited. To understand the influence of institutions one must compare what they were, are, and will be—that is, ascertain their condition at different times. . . .
>
> The prefect of the department of the Seine has published in several quarto volumes a *Statistique de la ville de Paris*, which gives information from which publicists have already drawn consequences of the highest interest. The facts and figures to be found in works of this kind can be infinitely multiplied, but by their very abundance they should be accepted with reservations. If similar statistical description were to be made for all places, and all possible facts included, men would have to yield their place to books; but who could buy them, and who could read them? . . .
>
> It is thus an important consideration that statistics should concern itself with a restricted field. This requires some explanation.
>
> Almost no conclusion can be drawn from a document made known only once haphazardly. If a document is published at a certain point in time on the population of a country, its provinces, and principal cities, it may satisfy curiosity but it loses veracity as soon as the population has changed, and can be of no use in the choice of means to improve conditions in the country. To be useful, such information and the presentation of accompanying circumstances must be repeated for several successive years. Only then can we see whether diminution of population coincides with the levy of certain taxes, or whether an increase of population ordinarily goes with the opening of communications, improvement of roads, more uninterrupted navigation on rivers and canals, or introduction of a new crop such as potatoes. We are then in a position

to infer cause and effect. If data are to be published successively every year, or every ten years, and if the same subjects are to be shown with changes brought by time and circumstances, we must restrict ourselves to essential points of information. In a word, statistical publications to be useful must be periodical works, and it is not possible for a periodical frequently renewed to be very extensive.

But who shall tell us what the essential points of information are, the facts that are important or from which important deductions can be made, those that help us to foresee future events, or can instruct us on our wishes and our fears? To identify such facts it is indispensably necessary to know the physiology of that living and complex being called *society* and to understand the organs by which it acts and preserves itself. Now the physiology of society is *political economy* as understood and cultivated in our time. We know by analysis the nature of different organs of the social body; experience shows the results of their action; hence we can decide on the points to which we should direct our observations so that consequences can be drawn. It can thus be said that *political economy is the foundation of statistics*, a proposition quite different from the common opinion that statistics is the foundation of political economy.

Statistics can announce a fact, but cannot explain it. Those who attempt an explanation without understanding the economy of societies are victims of an absurdity. To claim that facts ascertained by statistics are the foundation of political economy is equivalent to claiming that the quantity of spirits produced by distillers is enough to teach us how the process of distillation works.

The best statistical tables furnish no light on many other questions. Do the fees collected by lawyers, surgeons, etc., form part of the general income of a nation, or do they not? Is there or is there not a double counting when the production of grain to fatten a beef animal and the value of the animal fattened by this grain are both included? Does the laundryman who earns 2,000 *écus* a year, without introducing the slightest new product into the world, introduce a new quantity into the income of society? These questions are all susceptible to rigorous solutions.

Should it then be concluded that statistics can render no services to political economy? Such a conclusion would be too absolute. Statistics does not reveal the connection between facts, but by letting us see the successive course of several phenomena it can throw light on their reciprocal action; it can help to confirm truths of which the proof results from our study of the nature of each thing. If, for example, we can conclude from the nature of things that a tax levied on one kind of productive operation increases the cost of production, makes the product more expensive, and other things being equal diminishes the amount of that product which is produced and consumed, and so diminishes the production, enjoyments, and wealth of the country, this truth is confirmed by the statistics on consumption of sugar in France, which show that under Bonaparte only 14 million pounds of sugar were consumed in France each year, while in the following years the annual consumption was over 80 million.

It is also necessary to have statistical data that inspire some confidence. But when we know the manner in which the data are sometimes collected it is impossible to have much faith in them. Writers copy from each other. Each cites his predecessor as an authority, but on what did the predecessors depend?

After noting weaknesses in this respect in even the most careful writers, such as Lavoisier, Arthur Young, and Patrick Colquhoun, Say expresses doubt on official figures also:

What is worse, official documents are no more reliable than others. One ministry reports the floating debt at 250 millions; another offers proof that it was 800 millions at the same time. A minister of finance tells the legislature that the sums due to the Treasury reach 311 millions, which will appear as receipts on subsequent budgets as they come in; but they do not appear there at all. . . .

The vanity of peoples misleads them, even more than their interests, in statistics said to be based on incontestible truths. A British journal, putting the industry of Great Britain and the rest of the world in parallel columns, so as to give a grand idea of the former, claims that the amount of British cotton manufactures could not be achieved by sixty-two continents as large as Europe without Britain. We are supposed to believe that one Briton has sixty-two times the industrial capacity of any other inhabitant of the globe. And how do the authors support such a ridiculously inflated proposition? They compare the area of the whole earth with the area of Great Britain, and by distributing over this vast surface the amount of cotton manufactures in Great Britain, they easily conclude that, for every square mile, only one sixty-second as much cotton is produced as in Great Britain. By this method the industry of France, Belgium, Holland, Germany, etc., cannot seem to be very brilliant, when spread over the empty or thinly inhabited interior of the Americas, the sands of Arabia and the Sahara, along with Siberia and Lapland, in places where indeed not much cotton manufacture is to be found.

At this point Say has a footnote saying that the British journal whose absurd statistics he cites is the *Quarterly Review*, and then:

It is true that this is a Tory journal, but so far as national vanity is concerned the Whig journals are no better. See the ridiculous articles in which the *Edinburgh Review* compares the state of science and letters in France and England. In its number for July 1819 it claimed that an Englishman reads fifty times more newspapers and magazines than a Frenchman, from which it would follow that if a Frenchman spent a quarter of an hour each day in reading such papers an Englishman would spend his entire life.

Say next passes on to what would become known as a census. The word was then new. European governments had made population counts since the seventeenth century, but only sporadically, or locally, or for occasional particular purposes. The United States constitution of 1787 called for a decennial census as a basis for apportioning representation in the new lower house of Congress. The first American census was taken in 1790, and may have been the first legally required periodic census in any country, but the constitution does not use the word. It uses the word "enumeration," and Say in the 1820s uses the French equivalent, *dénombrement*. He begins by surveying attempts at counting population before authorized periodic and nationwide censuses became the rule.

One would be tempted to think that the number of inhabitants in a town or a region is susceptible to expression with tolerable exactitude. It would seem that the number of persons is a positive fact easy to ascertain. On the contrary, nothing is so difficult. We are dealing here not with inert matter, lacking in will, but with living beings animated by needs, tastes, interests, and passions that keep them constantly active. The problem is to establish their existence in civilized and hence populous places, at a specific moment because their number is always varying. Hence several agents must be employed at the same time, among whom some may be negligent or inaccurate. Some persons may be counted twice, and some may be overlooked.

Hence various methods have been tried for estimating the number of inhabitants of a country without directly counting them. One method, for example, has been to determine the number from the observed consumption of wheat; but apart from the fact that the same number of people buys and consumes much less when prices are high than when they are low, what calculation can be based on the consumption of a people like the French, half of whom almost never eat wheat bread, and are nourished by barley, rye, buckwheat, chestnuts, maize, beans, and potatoes, not to mention variable proportions of pork, rabbit, and butcher's meat often accidentally mixed in with these? . . .

It is evident that the best calculations so far attempted for the size of a population are essentially imperfect. The only good method is enumeration, but this method while it is the most accurate is the most difficult of all. An enumeration must be supported by the public authorities. Otherwise the heads of families and even of whole communities might refuse to give the indispensable information; the numbers would be unknown of persons in religious and civil communities, hospitals, and prisons; and even with the aid of authority the truth is not easy to discover. Where citizens are subject to a head tax or personal services such as the levy of troops, the heads of families will make imperfect declarations. Public officials themselves sometimes disguise the truth. I am told that the prefect of one French department (the Hérault), though the capital town of his department had only 29,000 inhabitants, was clever enough to report a figure of 35,000 by including a neighboring commune in the town. Those looking for a cause of this anomaly noted that the salary of our prefects is higher in proportion to the population of their place of residence. . . .

He cites the United States and the city of Glasgow as places where an "enumeration" is well documented, and concludes by listing the matters on which useful statistics can and should be obtained. Boundless and aimless information should be avoided; statistics should be "reduced to essential data," but these essential data on important matters are nevertheless of many kinds, and should be published either annually or every ten years.

It seems to me sufficient to publish once every ten years the numbers that can only be obtained at considerable expense and with much care, as well as averages for several years in which unusually high or low and hence false evaluations are not shown.

In decennial statistics the first chapter should be on population as found by an effective enumeration. . . .

The numbers of births, marriages, and deaths can easily be put in annual reports, or *statistical yearbooks*, because these numbers can be obtained from the required public registers, which are all the more accessible and authentic because they are recent, and anomalies can be corrected by averages over ten years in a decennial publication. The same applies to important products such as wheat. These quantities are always uncertain, and their annual variations can be smoothed over by publishing the average production for ten years.

Once every ten years is often enough, strictly speaking, for reporting the extent of land under cultivation in wheat, for growing fruits and vegetables, and for forests, meadows, and vineyards. . . .

The counting of beasts such as horses, asses, mules, horned and wool-bearing animals, as of population, need take place only every ten years. This is enough for knowing whether the change is progressive or retrogressive. . . .

Since a statement of receipts and expenses, commonly called a budget, under a representative government must be known to the legislature every year, it seems that such figures, or at least their totals, should appear in annual statistical yearbooks. . . .

It would be enough every ten years to report on certain physical facts of importance for the fate of humanity, but whose effects become apparent only after a lapse of time, such as how the removal of trees may affect annual rainfall. The quantity of water flowing in rivers can be not only seen by direct observation but calculated with sufficient exactness. The number of roads and their condition of viability, as well as the condition of navigable rivers and canals, also deserves inclusion in decennial statistics, for facility of communication and hence access to markets are among the principal elements in national wealth.

A chapter in decennial statistics that I regard as very important . . . is the *average price of objects of consumption*. It is known that nations are rich insofar as articles of consumption are cheap and abundant, and that these two words are only the expression of the same fact. Hence, among facts, prices furnish the most light on the condition of a people. I know that prices are significant only when the value of money, or of precious metals, is known; but the price of many objects, especially those of general consumption, offers one of the best means of knowing the value of precious metals themselves. . . .

The minerals of which it is most important to know the annual production are first of all *coal*, since heat is the most widely used of physical agents and wood cannot be reproduced as fast as the arts consume it; then *iron*, the most widely employed metal; then *salt*, etc. . . .

Say's article on statistics runs off at the end into an ever more hasty series of thoughts, as if he were pressed by a deadline at the *Revue encyclopédique*, but concludes with a characteristic bow to civilization and expectation of progress.

Yearbooks are appropriate for making known certain articles that are taxed, such as the number of periodicals; the number of national and private schools, and sometimes the number of their pupils; the judgments rendered in criminal cases; and even certain remarkable if merely curious events such as the fall of meteors from the sky.

In reporting annual deaths it is essential to note the age of the deceased, and so far as possible the malady that caused it, as also his occupation. These details make it possible to understand the influence of occupation on length of life; and the average length of life is the surest index to the condition of peoples. We know from data furnished by statistics, very imperfectly to be sure, that the average duration of human life has considerably increased in the last century or two, from which we can conclude that the well-being of the human race has become greater in most civilized states; but the statistics of the future will give our successors more precious and exact ideas on this subject.

We find an article by Say on a much broader subject than statistics in the *Revue encyclopédique* of 1828. It is a veritable exercise in world history, entitled "On the influence of the future progress of economic knowledge on the fate of nations."

A reader of Say's other writings may feel a certain disappointment on perusing this ambitious effort. The "fate of nations" is seen to depend in general terms on the presence or absence of enlightenment, progress, and civilization. The foil or opposite to political economy is ignorance and barbarism. The time had not yet come for argument against a developed socialism, the common ownership of the means of production (Babeuf had been marginal and was forgotten) or centralized planning in a command economy. We hear again Say's insistence that political economy is a science, but we might have expected a fuller statement of specific economic ideas that he had expressed elsewhere. He says nothing of the role of the state in providing reliable money to facilitate exchange, and an infrastructure of elementary schooling and of roads, canals, and harbors for transport and communication. There is nothing on the importance of the entrepreneur, and only a few remarks on how variation of prices in a free market offers a guide to productive investment.

He does reassert what he had said since the *Treatise* of 1803 (and what other economists were saying) on the legitimacy and importance of interest, meaning both a well-understood self-interest and the general interest of society. He sees such interest as a restraint upon the "passions," that is, the frenzy, ferocity, and delusion of religious persecution, wars of conquest, love of glory, and ostentatious grandeur. He thus illustrates that interaction between "the passions and the interests" to which the American economist Albert Hirschman has called attention.

His article on economic knowledge and the fate of nations begins:

> The social body has its laws, like the human body, laws that result from its nature, laws that man has not established and has not the power to abrogate. For managing either our own or the public affairs we have a keen interest in knowing these laws, so as not to wear out our strength against insurmountable obstacles and to benefit from the assistance that these laws can give. These are the laws that *political economy* proposes to discover and expound. But I think that applications of it have been misunderstood through failure to make an important distinction. . . .

The distinction to be made is in the different meanings of "interest," or between a purely selfish interest whereby one person gains while another loses, and the interest of society as a whole whereby the best interests of all members of society are most effectively promoted.

> Political economy, by making us understand the laws by which good things are created, distributed, and consumed, tends to promote the preservation and well-being not only of individuals but also of society, which without it would show only confusion and pillage.
>
> Societies, it is sometimes said, have managed to go on without a knowledge of political economy, and since they have so long done without it they can still do so. It is true that the human race grew up in ignorance. But the social body, like the human body, contains a vital force that surmounts the harmful effects of barbarism and passions. The personal interest of one private person has always raised an obstacle against the personal interest of another, and people have been forced to produce wealth when they could no longer take it by robbery.
>
> But clearly a system of opposing force by force is only a prolongation of barbarism, putting individuals and then whole nations into a permanent rivalry, productive of hatreds and public and private wars, for which complex laws and treaties and contrived balances of power have provided no adequate remedy. Like a pirate crew, each people had to think only of depredations, except in fighting among themselves over division of the booty, and then starting new violence to satisfy new needs.

He next surveys the "sad spectacle of history." In ancient times peoples slaughtered each other, and even their leaders and philosophers had no idea of the public good, since we see

> Lycurgus tolerating theft and ordering leisure, Cato not blushing to be a slave merchant, and Trajan staging festivals in which he had 10,000 gladiators and 11,000 animals killed.
>
> I say nothing of the barbarism of the middle ages, feudal anarchy, and religious proscriptions, a universal ferocity in which the conquered were always miserable without the conquerors being happy. . . .

But more recent times have been hardly better. Wars have been fought to capture a town or province, or gain an advantage in trade, or acquire colonies and then hold them in subjection.

These horrors of history are to be relieved by a newly found social science, and especially by its teaching of a beneficent freedom of international trade.

> But as soon as the conviction spreads that the growth and prosperity of one state does not come at the expense of another, and that new means of a state's existence and prosperity can be deliberately created,

and as soon as we can show how this creation can be effective and that the progress of one people is not harmful to the progress of another, but on the contrary is favorable to it, then the nations can find a more certain, more productive, and less dangerous means of existence, and each individual instead of groaning under the burden of public woes enjoys his share in the progress of the body politic.

That is what can be expected from a more widespread knowledge of the resources of civilization. Instead of founding public prosperity on brute force, political economy founds it on the well-understood interest of human beings.

At this point Say has a footnote, observing that these resources of civilization are not yet well understood by either governments or private persons, since there are "in the most civilized countries of Europe so many disparities between cities and in rural places so many cabins that resemble the huts of savages rather than the habitation of civilized people." But there is hope for the future.

Already, for several years, Europe has begun to be ashamed of its barbarism. As we have become more concerned with correct ideas and useful labor the examples of ferocity have become more rare. Wars have gradually been fought with less useless severity and less disastrous consequences; torture has been abolished among civilized peoples; and criminal justice is less arbitrary and less cruel. It is true that these happy effects are due more to the general progress of enlightenment than to a more improved knowledge of social economy. This form of knowledge is often entirely foreign to the most brilliant minds. Hence many desirable reforms are very recent, and many others are far from being accomplished.

If nations had not been, and were not even now, infatuated by the balance of trade and the idea that one nation can only prosper by detriment to another, fifty years of wars in the last two centuries could have been avoided, and our various peoples would not be shut up, each in its pen, by armies, police agents, and customs collectors, as if the intelligent, active, and peaceful element in the nations had no other aim than to do wrong. We are still every day victims of the past. . . . The more we study the more we are convinced that all our forms of knowledge date only from yesterday, and that perhaps more will date only from tomorrow.

What we need then is education, and especially education in the art of living in society. If the study of political economy could be made more reliable, and easy enough to be part of everyone's education, and if it could be achieved before the age of entering upon an occupation, we would have pupils exerting a greater and more favorable influence on the destinies of their country, whether called to public functions or remaining in private life. A nation is hardly advanced if it regards the evils it endures as necessities to be accepted when sent by fate, like violent storms and hailstones. No doubt some of our evils arise from our condition and the nature of things, but most of them are of human creation. On the whole, man makes his own destiny; and we know the consequences of the apathy and fatalism of Oriental peoples. . . .

So as not to be duped by charlatans or victimized by private interests, the public needs to know what its own interests are. Where public opinion is enlightened the government is obliged to respect it. The influence of public opinion is such that a government cannot keep up enforcement of a law if public opinion is against it. . . .

A parallel suggests itself between these views and a later scientific socialism as derived from Karl Marx: the past has been a story of poverty, inequality, and injustice; a new science of society is now available to produce social harmony and more equitable distribution of wealth; the change will be revolutionary in effect but need not be violent, since it may be accomplished by a peaceable takeover, whether by the proletariat in the one case or by a more enlightened public opinion in the other. But the parallel fails when Say goes on to argue that the desired goals are best met by representative government with assurance of equal rights— it would not occur to him to call all this "democracy." He grants that a society may sometimes prosper briefly under a "despotic" rule.

But it is not to be imagined that a despotism, even an enlightened one, can make a nation flourish as much as a regime in which national interests are consulted above all else. A nation, like a ruler's court, can be ignorant, poorly educated, and dominated by its passions, but it always really wants the public good. It has a direct interest in putting enlightened and honorable men into important positions. Where there are castes and privileged bodies no merit is necessary for reaching a higher place; the category a man is in suffices for his advancement. Under the regime of equality men are judged by other rules; they are classed according to their merit.

In such a regime those legislators and officials who know nothing of political economy run the risk of being assimilated to charlatans who, knowing nothing of the structure of the human body, undertake cures and operations that cause the sufferer's death, or expose him to infirmities sometimes worse than death. An ignorant person in power should be detested even more than a charlatan, if the ravages caused by their ineptitude are compared. . . .

We have grounds for applauding the rapid progress made by social science in the course of one generation. Much more progress will be made in the future. The best instructed men of each nation will move forward like pioneers in North America, and labor will follow to clear the land and repel the savages whose power declines every day. A few old and majestic trees will succumb in this march of nations, but in their place prosperity will seat itself beneath a more refreshing shade.

Social improvement will proceed more soundly as the task of watching over general interests becomes an occupation in itself, as a consequence of the division of labor, brought on by more numerous populations, more extensive needs, and more complicated interests. Only representative government can meet the needs of society, and such a government, by providing the necessary security and opening the door to desirable improvements, is itself a powerful means of prosperity. It will be adopted everywhere in the end; or a nation so retarded as not to want it will remain behind all the others, like a lazy or awkward soldier who stumbles as his troop marches forward and finds himself jostled and left behind by his comrades. . . .

Only political economy makes known the true ties that bind men in society. While discrediting old institutions it brings new force to good laws and good jurisprudence. It sets property on its true foundations, and shows its relation to personal abilities, new inventions, and particular groups. It explains the principles of law on questions arising from the interest on capital and from incomes from land, manufacturing, and commerce. It sets forth the conditions for a legitimate market, that is, the conditions in which price is either the measure of a genuine exchange, or the measure of nothing. It makes clear the importance of the arts, and the laws required for their practical applications. Has not lithography recently entered into our legislation? And if the time were to come when we can fly in the air, would we not need different laws from those we now have on enclosed places, passports, and import duties? . . .

Next comes a summary of practical advantages to the individual, especially concerning the value of foresight, such as he had outlined in lectures at the Conservatory, and finally a conclusion in a long and vivid figure of speech.

Knowledge of political economy has other advantages for those who possess it, quite apart from relations with the public. In many cases this knowledge supplements one's own experience, which can be costly and is often acquired at a time of life when it is no longer needed. . . . The consequences of circumstances in which we live, which ordinary people cannot suspect, are easily foreseen by whoever knows how to relate effects to causes. In any occupation it is a great advantage to have a more or less perfect, more or less accurate anticipation of the future. If I am a merchant, my gains and losses will depend on my opinion, more or less correct, of the future price of things. If I am a manufacturer, it is important for me to understand the effects of competition by other producers, of the distance of places from which my raw materials come and of places where I dispose of my products, and of the influence of means of communication and choice of processes in production.

In general, it results from the study of political economy that it is best in most cases for men to be left to themselves [laissez-faire!] because it is thus that they reach a development of their faculties; but it does not follow that they cannot benefit from knowing the laws that preside over this development. . . .

The grand concluding metaphor is reminiscent of Plato's cave, except that it ends with the magic word "progress."

We can represent a people ignorant of the truths proved by political economy under the image of a population obliged to live in a vast underground cavern, in which all the things necessary for life are also included and are to be found. Only the darkness prevents the cave-dwellers from finding them. Each person, in his need, searches for what is necessary to him, misses the object that he most hopes for, or crushes it underfoot without noticing it. Each calls upon, looks for, and cannot locate anyone else. There is no agreement on what each wants to have. Each grabs something for himself, or damages it; they maul each other. All is violence, confusion, and havoc—when suddenly a ray of light penetrates the cavern. They are embarrassed by the jumble they have created; they see that each can obtain what he desires. They understand that good things multiply in proportion as they come to each other's aid. Such is the image of a people plunged in barbarism, and of a people when it is more enlightened. And we shall be such a people when further progress, henceforth inevitable, will have come about.

Say's last years were a time of both triumph and tragedy. He brought out a fifth edition of his *Treatise* in 1826. He was greatly respected, and his books continued to be widely sold and translated. But he began to suffer from an illness that his son and editor remembered as a "nervous apoplexy," of which we can form no clear idea but which made his work more difficult and interrupted. After almost forty years of a happy marriage he lost his wife in 1830. Depressed as he was, he could welcome the revolution of 1830, when liberals like himself became more influential. They created a chair in political economy at the College of France, the summit of French intellectual excellence, and Say became its first incumbent. He barely missed election to the National Institute; he had been too young for it in 1803, when Bonaparte suppressed its class in Moral and Political Sciences, and when this class was restored in 1832 he was on his deathbed.

It is fitting to conclude these pages with excerpts from his opening lecture to his course at the College of France for the academic year 1832–33. It was delivered only a few weeks before his death. He was sixty-five years old, and anyone of such an age is likely to repeat himself, but his strength was ebbing, and a reader of this book may see in the lecture a somewhat rambling restatement of what he had said before. It was no doubt a fresher experience for his hearers at the College of France, which drew a different audience, whether more fashionable or more seriously scientific, from those who attended the Conservatory of Arts and Trades or read works on economics.

The lecture shows some interesting features. Say uses the terms political economy, the economy of society, and the economy of nations almost interchangeably, as if what are now called economics and social science were much the same thing; and this may well have been true at that time, when political science concentrated on constitutional arrangements and history, and sociology did not exist. We are told again that political economy is a moral science, but a true science because it is based on observation of the "nature of things," a term that recurs constantly, and means rejection of "system." The word "system" is used to characterize the misplaced abstraction, or *a priori* methods, for which he criticizes some of his predecessors, and also to dismiss invented and planned societies, which he sees in utopias written in the past and in projects of some contemporary reformers, the emerging socialists, for the future.

After preliminary observations Say addresses his audience at the College of France in 1832 as follows. All the italics are his.

> . . . It is first of all to be seen that the condition of men, their happiness or unhappiness, depends on circumstances of which some are in the moral order, that is, their behavior, and others in the political order, that is, the constitution of society and the way in which it is regulated. This is what puts political economy among the *moral and political* sciences. For a long time it formed part of political science, and writers of the middle of the last century saw little difference between *economic* and *political* questions, or between the organization of the powers of the State and questions relating to wealth and the means available, in greater or lesser abundance, by which nations and individual persons subsist and maintain themselves. But it then became evident that these two things depend on essentially different principles. It was noted that despotic governments might enrich their subjects, and popular governments keep their peoples in poverty; hence (guided by experience that made the nature of things better understood) there was a separation between these two kinds of knowledge. For political economy the

economists of the eighteenth century used the term *Physiocracy* (meaning natural government) until the arrival of Adam Smith, who called it an *Inquiry into the Wealth of Nations.*

This new term being thought a bit long and cumbersome, there was agreement on replacing it with the words *Political economy*, that is, the *Economy of society*. . . .

If we look briefly at human societies in general we can say that the primary and most natural of all societies is the family. Under civilized conditions we find other associations whose object is the pursuit of some common interest, such as societies for commerce, but these are not political societies. This latter term, in the language of science, is used especially to designate those large associations commonly called *Nations*, which arise from geographical convenience, or from having the same language, from the need of supporting themselves, or on occasion for defense against common dangers. . . .

There are many such "nations," including hunters and pastoralists in the interior of the Americas and in Arabia and Tartary; they have the rudiments of civilization, which are however not relevant to our present purpose.

Let us then turn to societies called (perhaps prematurely) *civilized peoples.* If they have not yet reached the degree of civilization of which man is capable, or all the tranquillity and well-being that civilization can produce, at least theirs is the most advanced civilization reached up to the present, and the only one on which we can profitably reason.

At first glance we see in civilized peoples only a confused mass of human beings wearing different costumes, equipped with diverse instruments, and changing their location or moving without changing place. If we look further into the purpose of their thoughts and actions we see that most of them are seeking subsistence for themselves and their families with varying degrees of enjoyment.

How do these individuals and their families subsist? By consuming things capable of supporting life or making it agreeable. . . .

Men eventually learned that it is less profitable to harm than to help one another. And since their needs are various, after learning how to obtain, create, and produce useful things, each in his own way, they engaged in exchanges. While the farmer raised grain or livestock for the merchant, the merchant brought groceries to the farmer; while the artisan prepared fabrics to clothe the magistrate, the magistrate provided security for the artisan.

It was long thought that the essence of the political body was in the government, that the social order was a work of art, and that wherever this order showed imperfections or disadvantages there was some fault of foresight or understanding on the part of the law-making authority, or some negligence or perversity on the part of officials charged with operating this complex machine. Hence came plans for imaginary societies such as the republic of Plato, the utopia of Thomas More, the Oceania of Harrington, and others more recent.

We have here, in this lecture at the College of France in 1832, one of Say's few references to what we now see as early socialist writings. The word "plans" above is Say's own, *plans de sociétés imaginaires*. His son Horace tells us that his father, toward the end of his life, became disturbed by such newly formulated ideas but refrained from trying to discuss them. Say probably had in mind the publications of Saint-Simon and his followers in the 1820s, and the spread of such ideas during and after the revolution of 1830. Say's text continues:

> Each thought himself able to replace a defective organization with a better one, without considering that in societies there is a *nature of things* that does not depend on human will, and which we cannot arrange according to our own wishes.

We must therefore, he says, have recourse to political economy, which fortunately has recently been gaining ground. In the following paragraph the reference to England cannot be to Oxford and Cambridge; Say must have had in mind John McCulloch, whose professorship he had mentioned in his article of 1828 on the new University of London, or possibly Malthus, who had long taught a course at the college operated by the East India Company for its own personnel. In any case, Say notes with satisfaction:

> Even despotic governments have not wished to remain exposed to the disadvantages of ignorance, and deprive themselves of the torches that give light to their fellow citizens. Chairs in political economy have been established in Germany, England, Italy, and even Spain. Princes destined to wear crowns have studied this science, and I have no doubt that as the solid bases on which it rests become better known it will be propagated more rapidly.
>
> I have said, Messieurs, that it rests on experience, that is, on the observation of facts and on the consequences deduced strictly from these same facts.
>
> On this matter I may make a remark already made in my *Treatise on Political Economy* since its earliest editions. It is that there are two kinds of facts that should serve as our guides. There are *things that exist*, and *events that happen*. The nature of things that exist is of the first kind. Gold is heavier than lead; that is a fact. The quantity of gold entering

France this year is of so many kilograms; that is a fact of another kind. It is an event that happens. Both kinds of facts can be established by experiences and observations of greater or lesser certainty, and are incontestable in greater or lesser degree.

When we wish to draw a conclusion from one or several facts it is indispensable to have a sound knowledge of the nature of things relative to both. It must be proved that the fact given as the cause has really produced the effect attributed to it, and that the nature of the thing given as the result allows for such an influence.

We must not be like that African monarch who had never seen ice. A Dutch captain was wrecked on his coast, and as he talked with the king about his country he told him how water, in a certain season, became so hard that people walked on the rivers with dry feet. The king thought that the Dutchman was making fun of him, and was inclined to hang him. The poor captain might have been hanged because His Majesty did not yet know the properties of water and the effects of cold. The nature of each thing and its properties are a fact, no less essential to know than an event, however positively determined.

Do you think there is much difference between this black Majesty and the inquisition in Florence, which imprisoned Galileo for saying that the sun stood still in the sky and that it was the earth that moved? Alas, how many have been persecuted for the wrong of having been right?

He goes on to repeat what he had said elsewhere on political economy as a moral science concerned with the nature of things, and on his eighteenth-century predecessors, the Physiocrats or "economists."

Then a little later Adam Smith, professor of moral philosophy at Glasgow, came to France and through his friend and compatriot, David Hume, was introduced to the best society in Paris and especially to the salon of the duchess d'Anville, mother of the duke of LaRochefoucault. Here he met Quesnay, Turgot, and all the leading economists. He had then already been long at work on the same subjects. His ideas spread. On his return to Scotland he withdrew to the little village where he had been born, and after ten years of study and reflection published his treatise on *The Wealth of Nations* in 1776, a work that contained enough truths to constitute a true science, but in which perhaps they are brought together with too much confusion, are too undigested and too poorly connected with each other to form a homogeneous whole and carry complete conviction.

Nevertheless, the origin of modern political economy can be dated from the publication of this book. I confess that on my visit to Glasgow

I greatly desired to see the upstairs room in which he lectured. I had the weakness to sit on his black leather chair, as if to receive an inspiration from which I might, Messieurs, communicate to you a few sparks. . . .

He proceeds next to put political economy in historical perspective, or rather to review those horrors and errors of the past that he had described, largely in the very same words and sentences, in his article on economic knowledge and the fate of nations in the *Revue encyclopédique* four years before. But he concludes on a new note, insisting that "civil society," as he calls it, is far more important than government. His recurrence to the model of the family, with a heavy emphasis on the role of the father, is his way of dismissing a paternalism in which persons in government are supposed to know more than those who are governed.

But as soon as the conviction spreads that one state may grow and prosper without doing so at the expense of another, and that its means of existence and prosperity may be deliberately created, and when we know how to bring about this creation, then feelings of hatred will come to an end and we will desire rather than dread the prosperity of another nation. The nations will know that there are means of existence more certain and more productive than those inherited from the ages of ignorance, and that each of the individuals of whom nations are composed may receive a larger share of ease, peace, and happiness.

Such, Messieurs, is what we can expect from a more widely diffused knowledge of the economy of nations. Instead of basing the public prosperity on hypothetical systems, or on an impulse to be received from governments, whatever they may be, we shall look for it in the well-understood interest of nations themselves. Nations are not nourished by the men charged with governing them, but by the men of who nations are made. That is where the *thought* and the *action* by which society subsists are lodged. It is a mistaken analogy to represent society as a family whose head is the father. The two things are essentially different. In the family it is the father who provides the means of subsistence; it is in his head that useful conceptions originate; it is he who procures the capital necessary to undertake a work. He is the one who initiates and directs the labor of his children, and who attends to their education and preparation for adult life.

In the social state it is the opposite. It is the governed who have the ideas on which the social body is based, who manage the enterprises and supply the capital to initiate them and the activity that makes them successful. It is the governed who study the laws of nature basic to all human labor, who practice the arts by which we live, and from whom come the incomes of all members of the nation from the most humble

to the most eminent. It is nature that creates the superiority of the father over his children, with greater power during their childhood because he is the more experienced.

In civil society both moral and political force are on the side of those
who have been called children (rather absurdly), for several million men
hardened to all kinds of labor, and possessing all kinds of knowledge,
are unquestionably stronger than the few hundred who govern them.

Nor is it an accurate picture, probably produced in government ante-
chambers, that represents the citizens as sheep and those set up to care
for the interests of the community as shepherds. Such an analogy can
only reduce human dignity to the condition of brutes. Political sheep-
folds are no longer suited to an age of maturity.

Such is the epigrammatic conclusion to Say's final introductory lecture.

No such laconic summary can close this book. What, indeed, can be
said? Perhaps, for one thing, that if Carlyle had read Say he would not
have found political economy such a dismal science, though he would
probably have still frowned upon it. It was a science, for Say, that would
bring about what he liked to call by the English word "comfort." The
purpose of production was consumption; an effective coordination of
capital, labor, and knowledge, motivated by a "well-understood" self-
interest, was to heighten the "enjoyments" of all members of society in
the future, if only they could be properly educated.

REFERENCES

GENERAL

SOME of Say's principal writings, together with a selection of his letters and short occasional pieces, were published sixteen years after his death in four volumes in Paris in 1848: *Oeuvres diverses de J.-B. Say*, edited by his son Horace Say, his son-in-law Charles Comte, and E. Daire. These four volumes were reprinted in Osnabruck, 1966, as volumes 9–12 in a collection called *Collection des principaux économistes*. In the following pages this work is cited as *Oeuvres diverses* in its reprinted edition. For other works by and about J.-B. Say, see the references below for separate chapters.

For Say's life and career, see the "Notice sur la vie et les ouvrages de Jean-Baptiste Say" by the editors of the *Oeuvres diverses*, vol. 4, pp. i–xviii. There is also the *Mélanges et correspondance d'économie politique: Ouvrage posthume de J.-B. Say publié par Charles Comte, son gendre*, Paris, 1833, much of which was reproduced in the *Oeuvres diverses* of 1848. For Say's life, see also J. Valynseele, *Les Say et leurs alliances*, Paris 1971, pp. 39–49, but the rest of this book is of less value for the present purpose, being an account of the advantageous marriages and hence genealogy of Say's ancestors and descendants. A paper called "Les mémoires de J.-B. Say" appeared in the Académie des sciences morales et politiques, *Travaux*, vol. 134, Paris 1890, pp. 377–90, but it is of little importance since the memoirs were very incomplete.

Say's place in the general history of economics is treated by J. A. Schumpeter, *History of Economic Analysis*, New York, 1954 (often reprinted), pp. 491–93, 555, and 615–18. See also the article by Thomas Sowell in the *New Palgrave Dictionary of Economics*, and at more length the older work by Charles Gide and Charles Rist, *Histoire des doctrines économiques depuis les Physiocrates jusqu'à nos jours*, 7th ed., Paris 1947, vol. 1, pp. 118–28. For Say's Law, see also the references to chapter 4 below. On other specific points, see references to relevant chapters below.

CHAPTER ONE
THE MILD REVOLUTIONARY

In 1989, in observance of the centenary of the French Revolution, a conference was held at Grenoble entitled "La Pensée Economique de la Révolution française." Thirty-five of the papers delivered at it were published in the monthly *Economies et sociétés*, vol. 24, Grenoble, 1990. They dealt with economic thought during the Revolution and with the economic policies and consequences of the Revolutionary and Napoleonic regimes. The paper most relevant to J.-B. Say was by Philippe Steiner, "Comment stabiliser l'ordre social moderne? J.-B. Say, l'économie politique et la Révolution française," pp. 173–93.

Three other articles are useful in placing Say and the development of political economy against the background of the Revolution: Thomas E. Kaiser, "Political Economy and the Idéologues," in *History of Political Economy*, vol. 12 (1980), pp. 141–60; and in the same journal, vol. 9 (1977), pp. 455–75, Michael James, "Pierre-Louis Roederer, Jean-Baptiste Say and the concept of *industrie*." More tangential to Say, but relevant, is Martin S. Staum, "The Class of Moral and Political Sciences, 1795–1803," in *French Historical Studies* 11 (1980), pp. 371–97. Political economy was one of the sections in this class at the National Institute, and Say would doubtless have become a member of it had it not been suppressed in 1803, the year when his *Treatise on Political Economy* was first published.

Say's pamphlet of 1789 is *De la liberté de la presse, par M. Sxxx, à Paris dans le temps de la convocation des Etats-Generaux de 1789.* Though anonymous, it is identified as Say's by his editors of the *Oeuvres diverses* (vol. 4, p. iv) and attributed to him by the standard bibliographers. Excerpts selected here for translation can be found as follows, according to the first few words of each excerpt.

Page

7	As for us	*Liberté de la presse*, p. 4
9	Having shown that	Ibid., p. 19
9	O you who make	Ibid., p. 27

On the *Décade philosophique* there have been two important works, both of which make frequent mention of J.-B. Say, who may be traced through their indexes. One is a French doctoral thesis written by an Englishwoman, Joanna Kitchin, *Un journal "philosophique": La Décade (1794–1807)*, Paris, 1965. The other is a huge five-volume thesis (in phototypescript) at the University of Lille by Marc Regaldo, *Un milieu intellectuel: La Décade Philosophique (1794–1807)*, Lille, 1976.

The portion translated here of Say's condensed life of Franklin appears as pp. lv–lxiii of *La science du Bonhomme Richard de Benjamin Franklin, précédée d'un abrégé de la vie de Franklin, et suivie de son interrogatoire devant la Chambre des Communes*, Paris, An II. Though the *abrégé* is anonymous, it is attributed to Say by the standard bibliographers and by Kitchin and Regaldo. For the complex story of Franklin's writings as known in France, see Paul Leicester Ford, *Franklin Bibliography: A list of books written by, or relating to, Benjamin Franklin*, Brooklyn, N.Y., 1899, pp. 179–85.

Say's writings for the *Décade philosophique*, with the translated passages identified by their opening words, may be found according to their dates in the *Décade* as follows:

Page

14	We find this work	30 Thermidor II, pp. 150–55
16	It may be useful	30 Pluviose VI, p. 354
17	Bureaucratic manners	Not located, but included as a contribution to the *Décade* by the editors of Say's *Oeuvres diverses*, IV, pp. 615–19
19	While our fourteen	20 Nivose III, pp. 488–91
21	Alas my dear Polyscope	10 Germinal IV, pp. 38–41

21	Popular spectacles	Ibid., pp. 41–42
23	This word	Ibid., p. 43
23	The constitution proposed	20 Messidor III, pp. 79–90
28	Among the institutions	10 Brumaire VII, pp. 198–212

CHAPTER TWO
THE SOBER UTOPIAN

Say's book is *Olbie, ou essai sur les moyens de réformer les moeurs d'une nation, par Jean-Baptiste Say, membre du Tribunat*, Paris, an viii de la Republique, 132 pp. It was reprinted in *Oeuvres diverses*, 4, pp. 581–615. The reprinted and original texts are identical, except that the reprint omits all the endnotes and most of the footnotes. References for translated passages are as follows:

Page		Oeuvres diverses, vol. 4	Olbie, ed. 1800
33	Now it is not by abstraction	584	ix
35	By moral behavior	585	1–2
36	A nation that has	588	9
36	Whoever would write	589	11
37	It is vain	589–90	11–14
37	In some modern colonies	592	19
38	I will now show	592–93	20–22
39	After the revolution	593–96	24–30
41	Our own Europe	596–97	30–32
41	For the working class	597–98	33–34
42	The leading persons	601–2	43–45
43	Until now I have	612–13	73–74
43	For this it is again comfort	613	74
43	They also had	613–14	74–77
44	A hundred other	614–	77–
45	Franklin's maxims and Say's conclusion	615	79–80

CHAPTER THREE
THE FRUSTRATED ECONOMIST

For this chapter, see items listed under General References and for chapter 1 above, and more specifically as follows:

Page		
47	The words spoken	*Archives parlementaires*, 2nd ser., Paris, 1862ff., 2, 90–91
49	In nations where	Ibid., III, 594; and *Oeuvres diverses*, 4, 198–202

52	It may be useful	*Traité d'économie politique* (1803), 1, i–iv
53	Political economy has	Ibid., vii–xi
54	It has almost always	Ibid., xxvii–xxix
55	Useful knowledge should	Ibid., xxxiv
55	It will seem	Ibid., xxxix
55	The dryness and obscurity	Ibid., xli
56	But the role	Ibid., 2, 435
57	Although several nations	Ibid., xliii–xlvi
58	Adam Smith thinks	Ibid., 1, 96–98
59	By real needs	Ibid., 2, 349
60	It is to be observed	Ibid., 2, 355
60	Louis XIV, toward	Ibid., 2, 406
61	I come now to colonies	Ibid., 1, 214–15
62	What is the effect	Ibid., 1, 215–19
63	I think I can affirm	Ibid., 1, 224–25
64	On profits of the slave	Ibid., 2, 247–49

The protest of a British antislavery society concerning the productivity of slave labor is Adam Hodgson, *Letter to M. Jean-Baptiste Say on the comparative expense of free and slave labor*, Liverpool, 1823. It was reprinted by the Manumission Society in the United States, New York, 1823.

CHAPTER FOUR
THE INNOVATIVE ECONOMIST

Excerpts as identified by their opening words:

Page

66	The mass of matter	*Traité d'economie politique* (1803), 1, 23–26
68	From the preceding	Ibid., 1, 27–28
68	People cannot make	Ibid., 1, 30–31
69	A doctor comes	Ibid., 1, 360–65
71	Profits of entrepreneur	Ibid., 2, 221–28
73	M. Storch is far	"Commentaires sur Storch" in *Oeuvres diverses*, 4, 303
74	Profits of the worker	*Traité* (1803), 2, 242–44
75	The extent of demand	Ibid., II, 175–79
76	In the number before	*Revue encyclopédique*, 23 (1824), 18–31; reprinted in *Oeuvres diverses*, IV, 250–52, 257–59

On Say's Law, in addition to works cited in General References above, see Thomas Sowell, *Say's Law: An Historical Analysis*, Princeton, 1972; William H. Hutt, *A Rehabilitation of Say's Law*, Athens, Ohio, 1974; Jurg Niehens, *A History of Economic Theory: Classic Contributions, 1720–1980*, Baltimore and London, 1990, pp. 110–15; and William J. Baumol, "Say's (at least) Eight Laws, or What Say and James Mill may really have meant," in *Economica* 44 (1977), pp. 145–61, reprinted in Marc Blaug, *The History of Economic Thought*, London, 1990.

On population see in the present book:

Page

79	By means of exchange	*Traité* (1803), 1, 386
80	If a population is limited	Ibid., 1, 390–96

For Say's years as a cotton manufacturer we rely on the recollections of his son Horace, one of the editors of the *Oeuvres diverses* published in 1848. Horace tells us that as a boy of ten he had assisted his father at the Conservatory of Arts and Trades in 1804, and presumably he lived with his parents in the Pas-de-Calais during the following years. See *Oeuvres diverses*, 4, x–xi. There is incidental information on Say in Serge Chassaigne, *Le coton et ses patrons, France 1760–1840*, Paris, 1991; and in William Reddy, *The rise of market culture: The textile trade and French society, 1750–1900*, Cambridge (England), 1984. Especially useful is an article by Charles Schmidt, "Jean-Baptiste Say et le Blocus Continental," in *Revue des doctrines économiques et sociales*, 4 (Paris 1911), pp. 148–54. Schmidt gives data on import duties on cotton, and publishes the letter (in the Archives Nationales) written by Say to the prefect of the Pas-de-Calais, of which extracts are translated here.

Say's letters to Jefferson of November 1803 and August 1814 are in the Jefferson Papers at the Library of Congress. Jefferson's replies are published in Lipscomb, ed., *The Writings of Thomas Jefferson*, 11, 1–3, and 14, 258–67. Say's letter of 1803 was published by Gilbert Chinard in *Jefferson et les Ideologues*, Paris, 1925, and a French translation of Jefferson's reply of March 1815 may be found in Say's *Oeuvres diverses*, 4, 397–403.

CHAPTER FIVE
THE COMMENTATOR ON ENGLAND

Say's *De l'Angleterre et des Anglais* was translated and published in English in 1816; I have, however, made my own translation. It is included in Say's *Oeuvres diverses* as edited in 1848, together with Say's own notes from the first edition of 1815 and further useful notes supplied by Horace Say, his son and editor. The following references are to the *Oeuvres diverses*, arranged by the first few words of passages in my translation.

Page

91	The long interruption	*Oeuvres diverses*, 4, 205–7
92	But while war	Ibid., 209–13, 16
94	The need for economizing	Ibid., 218–19
96	We saw at the beginning	Ibid., 221

97	The question of banknotes	Ibid., 222–23
98	There is another point	Ibid., 228–31
100	All these embarrass-ments	"Essai historique sur l'origine et les progrès de la souveraineté des Anglais aux Indes," in *Revue encyclopédique*, 23 (1824), 287. Also published as a separate pamphlet in English, London, 1824.
101	All this information	Ibid., 288–90
102	To find the source	Ibid., 293–95
104	In any case	Ibid., 298–99
105	A British admiral	"De l'absentisme, et ce que deviendra l'Irlande," in *Revue encyclopédique*, 40 (1828), 283–86
108	The English believe	Ibid., 289–90
108	This overflow of Irish	"Troisième rapport fait en 1827 à la Chambre des Communes d'Angleterre sur les emigrations et les colonisations," in *Revue encyclopédique*, 37 (1828), 396–98
110	The foundation of a university	"Fondation d'une université à Londres," in *Revue encyclopédique*, 39 (1828), 537–39.
112	For intervals between classes	Ibid., 540
112	So we have an immense	Ibid., 541–43
113	This new science	Ibid., 544–45
115	The living languages	Ibid., 546–47
116	The Tory Party	Ibid., 549

CHAPTER SIX
THE PROFESSOR OF POLITICAL ECONOMY

For Say's professorship of political economy, see, in addition to items cited in General References above, M. Ventré-Denis, "Sciences sociales et Université au 19ᵉ siècle: Une tentative d'enseignement de l'économie politique à Paris sous la Restauration," in *Revue historique* vol. 256 (1976), pp. 321–42; and A. Liesse, "Un professeur d'économie politique sous la Restauration: J.-B. Say au Conservatoire des Arts et Métiers," in *Journal des économistes*, 5th ser., vol. 46 (1901), pp. 3–22 and 161–74. Also useful are the concluding pages of M. S. Staum,

"The Class of Moral and Political Sciences, 1795–1803," in *French Historical Studies*, vol. 11 (1980), pp. 371–97.

Say's principal writings published from 1814 until his death in 1832 were three in number, listed below with full titles suggesting the audience for which they were intended, and with an indication of their successive editions and translations within his lifetime. Say remarks in a letter of 1829 (*Oeuvres diverses*, 4, 563) that he had in his own library translations of his works into fourteen languages. The translations shown below are as recorded in the printed catalogues of the Bibliothèque Nationale, the British Library, and the Library of Congress.

Nothing from these three works is included in the present book.

1. The second and following editions of the *Traité d'économie politique, ou Simple exposition de la manière dont se forment, se distribuent et se consomment les richesses, entièrement refondue et augmentée*, Paris, 2 vols., 1814, 1817, 1819, 1821, 1826. Translated into Spanish 1816, 1821; Italian 1817; English 1921, 1824, 1827, 1830; German 1814, 1830; Swedish 1823; Danish 1825. Since the first edition of the *Traité* (1803) was never translated into English, excerpts from it are translated in chapters 3 and 4 of the present volume.

2. *Catéchisme d'économie politique, ou Instruction familière qui montre de quelle façon les richesses sont produites, distribuées et consommées dans la société*, Paris 1815, 1821, 1826. Translated into Spanish 1816, 1822; German 1816, 1827; English 1816; Greek 1828.

3. *Cours complet d'économie politique pratique, ouvrage destiné à mettre sous les yeux des homme d'état, des propriétaires et des capitalistes, des savants, des agriculteurs, des manufacturiers, de négotiants et en général tous les citoyens, l'économie des sociétés*, par Jean-Baptiste Say, Paris, 7 vols., 1828, 1832; Italian 1833; German 1829.

References for the present chapter are as follows for passages beginning with the first few words.

Page

118	You have asked me	*Oeuvres diverses*, 4, 520
119	The systematic part	Ibid., 521
120	Hence badly conceived	Ibid., 523
121	The Government shows	Ibid., 133
122	The method that	Ibid., 141
124	Our nation, absorbed	Ibid., 428
125	As for your translation	Ibid., 430
126	I pass over	Ibid., 433
127	An important consequence	Ibid., 324
128	Since Storch persistently	Ibid., 336
129	three-quarters of his book	*Revue encyclopédique*, 25 (1825), pp. 577–79
130	For lack of canals	*Traité d'économie politique*, ed. 1814, 2, p. 286; ed. 1819, 2, p. 324; Eng. trans. 1821, 2, p. 240.

130	There is now much	*Oeuvres diverses,* 4, 234
131	One last step	Ibid., 237
132	The United States	*Revue encyclopédique,* vol. 13 (1822), 385
135	In the opinion of	Ibid., vol. 24 (1824), 5
136	The government therefore	Ibid., 8
136	But one commissioner	Ibid., 9
137	In the general assembly	Ibid., 16

The letter from President Boyer of Haiti is printed in the *Revue ency-clopédique,* vol. 24 (1824), 224–27.

Page

139	Everyone knows	*Revue encyclopédique,* vol. 35 (1827), 529
141	What is worse	Ibid., 537
142	It is true	Ibid., 537
142	One would be tempted	Ibid., 539
143	It seems to me	Ibid., 548
144	Yearbooks are appropriate	Ibid., 552
145	The social body	*Revue encyclopédique,* vol. 37 (1828), 14
146	Political economy by making	Ibid., 15
146	Lycurgus tolerating	Ibid., 16
146	But as soon as	Ibid., 17
147	Already for several	Ibid., 18
148	So as not	Ibid., 20
148	But it is not	Ibid., 27
149	Knowledge of political economy	Ibid., 30
150	We can represent	Ibid., 33
151	It is first of all	*Oeuvres diverses,* 4, 176
152	If we look briefly	Ibid., 179
152	Let us then turn	Ibid., 180
153	Even despotic govern-ments	Ibid., 184
154	Then a little later	Ibid., 188
155	But as soon as	Ibid., 192

INDEX

absenteeism, 105
Alexander I, tsar of Russia, 83
America. *See* colonies, United States
"America," "American," use of words in various languages, 137
American Colonization Society, 134–38
American language, 115
American Revolution, 12–13, 15. *See* United States
Amsterdam, 90
ancients and moderns, 21–22
arts, artistes, meaning of French words
Ashmun, 136
Athénée, 88, 117
Australia, 108, 109

Bacon, Francis, 34, 45
Bank of England, 96, 97
Bath, 91
Bentham, Jeremy, 66, 90, 100, 129
Biddle, Clement, 58, 125
Birmingham, 92
blacks, free, 134–38. *See* slavery; Liberia
Bonaparte, Napoleon, 33, 50, 52, 58, 61, 82, 87, 111, 126
Bridgewater, duke of, 131
Bristol, 92–92
Britain, Great, Say in, 5, 91; conditions in, 90–116; British hostility, 47, 49; misc., 120, 127, 131–32, 141
budgets, 49–51
bureaucracy, 17–19
Burke, Edmund, 27

Cambridge University, 110–12
Canada, 61, 108–9
canals, 129–34
Carey, Matthew, 126
Carlyle, Thomas, 156
Catholic Emancipation, 105
Cato, 146
censorship of press, 7–10, 52
census, 142–44
Charlottesville, Va., 41, 44
China, 103, 127
civil ("bourgeois") society, 52, 155–56

civilization, 104, 127–28, 135, 136, 152
Clavière, Etienne, 5, 10
Clay, Henry, 134
College of France, 118, 151–56
colonies, 37, 48, 61–65, 99, 134
Colquhoun, Patrick, 93, 98, 141
comfort, 22–23, 39, 43, 77, 156
Committee of Public Safety, 9, 25–26, 27
Condorcet, 79
Conservatoire des Artes et Métiers (Conservatory of Arts and Trades), 27–32, 81, 110, 117–18, 121–22
constitutions, French, of 1791, 50; of Year III (1795), 23–27, 50; of Year VIII (1799), 25, 28, 46
consumption, 68, 128, 156
Corn Laws, 96
Cousin, Victor, 124

debt, 93, 98–103
Décade philosophique, 6, 10, 17
declaration of rights, 24
Destutt de Tracy, 33, 129

East India Company, 98–104
economic development, 27–32, 117–19, 132. *See* entrepreneur.
Edinburgh Review, 113–14, 142
Edinburgh, University of, 111, 113
education, 35–36, 56, 147, 156
Egypt, 47–48
emigration (from British Isles), assisted, 108–10
England. *See* Britain
entrepreneur, 66, 70–74, 118–24; Say as entrepreneur himself, 81–82
Erie Canal, 129, 132–34

Franklin, Benjamin, 4, 11–17, 34, 45, 59, 60, 61, 108
freedom of the press, 6–10, 52

gain, dangerous love of, 40–41, 124. *See* interest
Galileo, 154
Garnier, translator of Adam Smith, 70, 76

Glasgow, 90, 92, 94, 143, 154
Grégoire, Henri (abbé), 27, 30–31
Guizot, François, 124

Haiti, 66, 137–38
Heliogabalus, 60
Hirschman, Albert, 145

Idéologues, 10, 33, 52
immaterial products (services), 66, 69–70, 80
India. *See* East India Company
industrial revolution, 3, 90, 95
inflation, 20, 94
Institute, National, 29, 33, 52, 150
interest, 53–54
interest, self (as morally good), 124, 128, 145
Ireland, 104–8

Jacobins, 19–20, 27
Jefferson, Thomas, 83–88, 134
Jullien, Marc-Antoine, 100

King's College (London), 110, 116

labor and labor unions, 71, 74–75
La Fontaine, 34, 45
laissez-faire, 79, 150
Lancaster system, 94
Lavoisier, 141
laws, avoidance of too many, 26, 70
Liberia, 134–38
Liverpool and Manchester Canal, 129, 131
Liverpool and Manchester Railway, 129
London University, 110–16
Louis XIV, 60
Louis XVIII, 83, 89
Lucullus, 60
luxury, 20, 42, 57–59
Lycurgus, 146

Macaulay, T. B., 112
Malaga, 117
Malthus, Thomas, 3, 79–80, 84, 117, 153
Manchester, 92, 108
Marx, Karl, 66, 148
mathematics in political economy, 55, 138
McCulloch, J. R., 107, 113
Mill, James, 61, 90–91, 100, 112
Mill, John Stuart, 100
Mirabeau, Marquis de, 10

moeurs, translation of, 34
money, 67, 91, 95–97
Monroe, James, 137
Monrovia, 137
monuments, 44

Nelson, Horatio Lord, 93, 102
New Zealand, 108

Olbia, 32–45, 59, 80
Oxford University, 110–11, 113

Physiocrats, 68, 152, 154
Place, Francis, 91
Plato, 44, 153
political economy as a science, 3, 52–54, 85, 117, 122–24, 140, 148, 151
political economy to be understood by everyone, 20, 36, 39–40, 44–45, 54–58
Polytechnique, Ecole, 110
Poor Richard's Almanac, 11, 14–15, 59. *See* Franklin
population, 79–81, 108
Prinsep, Robert, 125–26
productivity, 94, 130. *See* entrepreneur

Quarterly Review, 141
Quesnay, François, 154

railways, 95, 129–30
Revue encyclopédique, 76, 100, 104, 108, 129, 133, 134, 138, 145
Ricardo, David, 3, 91, 97, 117, 124
risk, 54, 73–74
Robespierre, 9, 24, 27
Rousseau, 35

Saint-Simon (social philosopher), 153
savings, 58–59
Say, Jean-Baptiste, background and career, 3–6; as entrepreneur, 81–83; idea of emigration, 83–88; writings, *passim*
Say's Law, 3, 66, 75–79, 81
Scotland, 107, 120. *See* Britain; Edinburgh; Glasgow
services. *See* immaterial products
Sismondi, J. C., 76–78, 129
slavery, 61–65, 86, 88–89, 134–38
Smith, Adam, as founder of modern economics, 51, 53, 65, 107, 112, 114, 120, 129, 151, 154; Say's first knowledge of, 5, 7, 90; Say's differences with, on "sav-

ings," 58; on "immaterial products" (services), 69; on slavery, 63; on "profits," 71
"social economy," 3, 110, 118, 125, 151
socialism, 57, 153
South Africa, 108–9
statistics, 138–45. See mathematics
steam engines, 32, 95, 129–30
Storch, Heinrich, 73, 127–29
subsistence theory of wages, 74

Tasmania, 109
Terror (France 1793–94), 5, 23, 27
theater, 19–21, 43
Thénard, L. J., 118
Thermidorian reaction, 19, 23
Tocqueville, Alexis de, 139
Trajan, 146
Treatise on Political Economy, 3, 33, 46, 51–89, 97, 114, 125
Tribunate, 34, 46, 49
Turgot, A. R., 63, 154

useless consumption, 58–60. See consumption; luxury; utility
United States, 4, 24, 37, 41, 49, 80, 92, 108; slavery in the, 61–65; Say's plan to emigrate to the, 83–89; English language in the, 115. See colonies; Erie Canal; Liberia
University College (London), 110–16
utility, 66–68, 120–21
utopia (perfected society), 22, 27, 34, 153. See comfort; Olbia
Utopia (Thomas More), 33

value, 66, 68–69, 119, 122, 130
Venice, 41
Versailles, 59
Voltaire, 34, 37, 128

Webster, Daniel, 134
Wellesley, Marquess of, 101

Young, Arthur, 141